Customizing Your Motorcycle

SHED-BUILT TO SHOW BIKE

Customizing Your Motorcycle

SHED-BUILT TO SHOW BIKE

Chris Daniels

THE CROWOOD PRESS

First published in 2018 by
The Crowood Press Ltd
Ramsbury, Marlborough
Wiltshire SN8 2HR

www.crowood.com

**British Library Cataloguing-in-Publication
Data**
A catalogue record for this book is available
from the British Library.

ISBN 978 1 78500 369 1 ✓

Frontispiece: A Honda NX650 big thumper
leaving my shed in style; weight saved by
dumping the rubbish turns it into a serious
twisty lane and town bike. And it looks good.

Typeset by Shane O'Dwyer, Swindon, Wiltshire
Printed and bound in India by Replika Press

contents

welcome to our world

A WONDERFUL WORLD

In a world of safety concerns and risk assessments, it is not easy to celebrate the individual. Sure, individualism can be expressed by dressing differently, becoming an explorer or just dropping out, but these methods can all impinge too much on daily life. As an alternative, many people buy mass-produced items they believe will make a statement of how they stand out from the crowd. Eventually, though, there comes a time when the ownership of off-the-shelf technology and cheap rubbish, manufactured by tiny hands in far-off countries, starts to become meaningless and trivial. This is a shame, as the world has much to offer in terms of enjoyment and enrichment, not all of which is to be found on a thumb-operated screen, but the real question is, how do you know where it is, and then, more importantly, how can you participate?

While there are no simple answers to these questions, for those with a desire to leave the sheep behind, who are blessed with gumption, and possess fair motor skills and opposable thumbs, a decent solution exists: take a standard motorcycle, throw away the garbage and build a custom bike!

Who could fail to be impressed by the coolness of a well-turned-out bike? Who would not appreciate the freedom of the open road (or field) on a machine that has been transformed, by someone

TOP LEFT: Shed-built Harley bobber, with a bold distinctive colour scheme created using spray cans, with stick-on vinyl Triumph logo. The air-filter cover was customized by drilling random holes and polished using a wheel in a drill press, with fine mesh secured on the inside with silicone rubber.
LEFT: The epitome of shed creativity? This lovely machine was built using a scooter as the basis and classic-car bodywork, to create a unique and practical custom for very little cost. Imagination and experimentation are two of the best tools in the customizer's arsenal.

using their imagination and hand skills, into an assertion of life? Hopefully within the following pages, a basic understanding of working on these lovely machines will be engendered, whilst the concepts of how to tailor them using readily available tools, equipment and ideas will be set out in an understandable and practical way. Most forms of transportation – cars, trains, and so on – are designed to move people about in maximum safety and with minimum fuss. What bikers are after is excitement, style and fun. Unfortunately, as the manufacture of bikes has become a massive business, the machines over the years have been (over) developed into catering for the lowest common denominator, designed to be mass produced.

UNIVERSAL CUSTOM

Basically, a motorcycle is an engine slung on a metal frame between two wheels and it is this simplicity that allows it to be light, nimble and easy to work on. Well, that was true when they first came out and it carried on for many years, allowing creative people to take the basic layout and expand on it. The

ABOVE: Classic shed customizing at its best: simple and sweet, Ben's old Triumph would not look out of place in a 1950s biker flick, outside a Paris wine bar in the 1960s or rolling into the car park of a modern design studio. All unnecessary stuff was binned and the old worn-out seat was replaced using an old leather jacket.

RIGHT: Definitely not shed-built, this shop-manufactured custom is a standard bike with lots of lovely bits stuck on. It requires no more input from its new owner than looking through a glossy catalogue and getting a cheque book out; the amount it costs would buy about fifteen second-hand classic runners.

manufacturers, seeing that there was a definite market for the 'individual' bike, set to with a vengeance to create mass-produced custom bikes; they have flooded the world with creations that range from the sublime to the ridiculous, capturing an audience that totally ignores the irony of purchasing a factory custom.

Consider the differences between the bikes of days gone by and the new wave of factory output; while this may appear to be an exercise in cynicism (or critical examination if you will), it is quite important to appreciate constructional evolution when choosing a bike to customize. The most appreciable difference is space, older bikes tend to have a lot more room around the engine, be skinnier and look lighter.

Newer bikes have been computer-designed to fill out all the spaces with cleverly located components, shiny gewgaws and acres of plastic; the result is often a stolid, boring and complicated machine devoid of character. Other obstacles on newer bikes are electronic and fuel systems, which can be a pain to organize. This is especially the case when going minimal, as many of them need computer control, or to be set up via a computer-controlled system.

It makes sense to use as your basis a bike that can actually be worked on at home, so the first piece of advice is this: do not buy some overly convoluted,

electronically controlled spaceship of a bike, but keep it simple and go classic.

DO IT YOURSELF

This book is not intended to be an instruction manual on exactly how to customize a particular bike; that is up to you. Instead, it will demonstrate and explain techniques that should help when working with bikes, engines and tools in general.

The basis for anyone working on mechanical objects must be grounded in the simple tasks of an average workshop; these used to be garnered at school or by finding out as a youngster on pushbikes and old wreckers. Unfortunately, the time of the ubiquitous garden shed full of the tools needed to keep the family vehicles and appliances running has gone; the drive to always buy newer and shinier stuff means that people don't look after things as they used to. A sweeping generalization, very vernacular and full of holes, but there's a truism in there somewhere – trust me.

The book will feature a couple of project bikes shown as examples, as well as pictures of interesting bits of bike and of bikes themselves, all of which will be included with a strong bias towards what I personally like or admire. The two are not always the same – it is easy to like a bike, without being impressed

by certain elements of it; on the other hand, clever engineering or details may exist on a bike that, to my senses, is a complete dog's dinner.

This brings up another point that is quite important to me but, from what I've seen, not everybody: aesthetic style. Now this is getting subjective, it's obvious we can't all like the same thing, and while that is almost the raison d'etre for customizing, it is quite difficult to say nice things about something that has as much attraction as a mangled gate.

What I will attempt is to describe why I like particular bikes, or how something mechanical quickens the heart, so when the inevitable matter of criticism occurs, be aware that it is not personal. In fact, not being keen on something means it won't be something I'll copy, thus preserving its individuality.

The details are not the details. They are the design.
CHARLES EAMES

IN THE RIGHT DIRECTION

Hopefully, you already have some idea about the type of bike you would like to be riding. There is no way you can be helped to choose without knowing what you find cool about bikes, where you live and how you plan to spend time out on the road. As a start, it is handy to try and identify these aspects, amongst all the other factors that have made you decide that this is the life for you.

The range of what can be termed 'custom bikes' is huge, with new sub-groups or designations constantly popping up, probably as a result of people's need to be part of an exclusive group, while still being able to explain how individual they are.

The original choppers were named thus simply because all the junk was 'chopped' to lighten the bike. This developed into a catchall title for almost any custom that made the bike different, with the difference sometimes going way over the top.

The most iconic of the choppers is Captain America, built for the film *Easy Rider*; recognizable by everyone, it is a beautiful bike of the era, only suited to the long, straight roads of America.

Once upon a time, many years ago, large numbers of very similar motorcycles were pushed off the new-fangled

Pepe's Moto Guzzi has a wealth of shed custom details: the brass and copper fitments, electrics box made from an old motor housing and rustic seat all give it a singular charm. Some might prefer more minimalism and tidiness in the routing of the cables and wires, but most are happy for them to be an integral part of the whole scheme.

factory production lines, intended to be an economic and efficient means of transport for the common man. This led to generations of working-class lads, and a few lasses, owning and, more importantly, maintaining machines. Unfortunately, those machines were generally slow, uniform and cheap, so the next logical step for many owners was to start to modify them.

After World War II, as men returned from the war with a different attitude to life, the invention of the lawless and disgruntled teenager, coupled with having spare money and leisure time meant things would happen. Being human, this invariably led to activities designed to be dangerous, but fun, so racing cars and bikes it was. While the car world went off on its own, and hot-rodding became the culture of customizing cars (ironically using the old vehicles and revelling in the retro styling), bikers were taking their machines

Timeless in its beauty, this old Sunbeam exudes the essence of shed, showing that true style is for ever. Try not to follow fashion trends; just make it high quality and with panache.

A 45 bobber cooling down after a blast round the dirt track; its modern spoked wheels sit well with the almost agricultural rawness of the design.

ABOVE: *A lesson in less is more: the ultimate tracker Harley XR is perfection in design and stance, with nothing that is unnecessary to its function.*

LEFT: *Marmite on wheels? Chops are either loved or hated and, the more extreme they get, the wider the divide. Even for those who are not keen, there is something to be admired in some of the crazy detailing. This one has everything going on – shiny bling is not a new thing.*

wide and high

The original bobbers had wide 'cowhorn' handlebars, carried through to flat-track racing. Motocross has a similar style, the leverage of the bar allowing a bucking and twitching front wheel to be held on course. It is simple physics, but it is useful to consider when choosing 'bars, as they do contribute to the way in which the bike handles and rides.

Norley: a shed-built frame based on the Norton Featherbed with a Buell engine. It is a formidable beast, but building one is actually quite affordable. The frame is hand-built to order and the engine just drops in, to create a great-handling café racer for substantially less cost than a new mid-range bike.

and modifying them for racing on dirt tracks, or anywhere with enough room to get up speed and, if lucky, go around corners. Thus the Bobber was born – low slung, with all extraneous metal-work, pillion seats and heavy silencers removed, and mudguards cut down or 'bobbed'. It was a style that eventually became synonymous with carefree youngsters, rebels and, in some instances, outlaws. This was captured in the film *The Wild One*, in which a squeaky-clean Marlon Brando customized his Triumph by sticking a gilt trophy on the headlight. His gang of 'rebels' fought the law and a grubby, drunken Lee Marvin, who rode a worn-in Harley bobber. For me, Marvin easily won the style stakes, and the level of cool he exuded was to colour my attitude towards biking for decades – and in a way still does. Brando's style, in his creakily new leather jacket, was not for me.

An enterprising bike racer with access to garage tools and welding gear could fairly easily make his machine suitable for straight-line speed, by lengthening the frame, chopping it and inserting tubes, to improve stability, and so on. Such modifications were then taken up by non-racers and this is how the 'chopper' was born. The 'standard' chopper evolved to have a Harley engine, forward control and extended forks – which necessitated stretching and raking the headstock – as well as a small tank and perhaps an interesting seat. They were basically altered drag bikes, light and nimble, but gradually became increasingly radical and lost all pretence at improving the handling. British engines were also used, and, when Japanese production started in earnest, these fell in nicely too, especially the lovely, dependable and fast Honda CB750. This was, and continues to be, one of the most popular form of

customized bike and the most easily recognized by non-bikers worldwide.

'Chopping', a term that really describes the sloughing of superfluous parts and weight from a bike, can cover a wide range of styles. However, the general idea is that, when a bike has been visibly altered from the standard, it has been 'chopped'. Such a loose definition allows those who do not want to reinvent the wheel every time someone puts a different seat on a bike or drops the bars of a scrambler, the easy get-out

of giving the name 'chop' to anything that is not recognizable as a café racer, tracker, scrambler or racing bike. In this book, where 'chop' or 'chopper' is used as a noun, it can refer to just about any other modded bike that looks substantially different from standard.

BACK IN ALBION

Meanwhile, over the Atlantic things were literally going in a different direction. Due to the miserable climate, lack of

Clean SR500, showing how minimal structural work and nice details can create a ridable and cool bike. The stepped silencer end, cute lights and chunky tyres on deep alloy rims look so right, while wide bars and a ribbed seat with sensibly placed pegs give a comfortable ride.

large dry areas big enough to race on and no stretches of 'highway' good or long enough to even consider owning a chopper, the Brits had to take to the winding, coarsely surfaced roads of the British Isles. No warm beaches, cool bars or secluded cabins to congregate in meant the Britbikers met up in local greasy spoons to drink warming tea, scoff sausage butties and organize blasts around the locale. For this a different style of machine was needed; one that could handle the coarse, cratered and twisting tarmac of the UK; the Café-Racer was born. Based upon road-racing bikes of the day, engines were tweaked, suspension and brakes upgraded, and the riding position altered with short 'clip-on' bars and rear-set controls; it was about speed, handling and looking cool.

Another branch of motorsport that provided inspiration for customized bikes was off-road – scrambling (now motocross), trials and enduro. This resulted in a thin nimble bike with a sit-up-and-beg riding position and high-level exhausts. Street scramblers were ideal for town and country, but less well suited to fast and long road work.

While it is possible to identify the sources of inspiration in the wide range of custom styles that the world is now blessed with – whether factory-produced or hand-made – often there is a melding or convergence of different styles. Although the best bikes tend not to hammer themselves into a niche, less imaginative owners, and those wishing to be part of a clique, usually adopt a definite name for their particular style. In this book, the aim is not to be too precious about this; get the ideas or details into an end product that is clearly yours, and then call it what you will. One important point is that customizing used to be about improving the bike whilst maintaining good aesthetics; it still is in many areas (obviously excluding the radical world of show bikes).

Looking back at the levels of prettiness, care and colour schemes of the original chopper, usually ridden by a cool outlaw figure, I'd offer that these bikes were the only form of creativity that was acceptable to the disenfranchised class of that era. Maybe that was part of my reason for building them: I couldn't afford new bikes, so tended to make my own out of whatever was available. As with many social pursuits

you had to (slightly) fit in with people or they wouldn't even talk to you, let alone ride, so you'd tend to follow the norm. Now the customized bike is an accepted part of culture, admired and embraced across age and class. Many enjoy this vicariously by buying an off-the-shelf 'custom'; for those who like authenticity, and the chance to get practical, the only real way is to be the builder and rider of your own personal machine.

TODAY

Fashions come round again, and there is now a resurgence in what could loosely be termed new bobbers, the 'Brat bike'. Basic machines are stripped

of standard components, have chunky tyres and skinny seats added, and are wheeled out as the new wave of customs. Opinion may be divided on these being classed as proper customs, but it's each to his own and as I'm only really here to offer advice, I'll try to keep the criticisms as objective as possible.

My personal advice to the budding shed builder is aimed toward making a ridable bike, one that can be used for what they're meant to do, having fun, looking cool, while staying safe. Just as great artists start by making recognizable works before stretching the boundaries, learn how to build a bike that works first, then if the urge demands, play around and create far-out customs.

Another 500 Yam shows an interesting take on the big single. This is how it is done, with no compromise – late nights in the shed fabricating the trick fairing and bodywork, and other details such as the headlight in a piston, snouty exhausts and lovely seatwork.

When manufacturers create a custom, the result is often a far cry from the cut-down ridable machine most riders desire. Here is a prime example of how not to do it: massive, ugly and with so much detail contributing nothing!

choosing your ride

THE BIKE

What bike should you use as a base for customizing? While it is obviously a very personal choice, there are a number of factors that will point you in the right direction. Of course, this advice will be redundant if you are already in possession of your very own dream machine.

Hopefully, you will have at least a rough idea of the style that you want to aim for; this, coupled with what you will be doing on it and where it will be done, will be the main factors when scouring the ads. Try to work out what you want from your bike and what customizing will do to it. Pictures of bikes and frames can be found online and printed off, and then used to sketch shapes and layout. For the tech savvie, it is possible to use photo-editing, drawing and design software to mock up a concept of the perfect bike, but it is important to keep it within the realm of what is achievable with your level of skills and funds.

Working on a first bike that is to be used daily, it makes sense to keep away from extremes, to make life easy. For example, a sit-up style is the easiest to cope with in town and off the beaten track. It also helps to choose a bike that will be lightweight, cheap and easy to work on. That first bike may be just the starting point; once you have made something decent from it, you will probably get the itch to do better next time, putting the first one up for sale in order to fund the next project.

The above is all very handy for a bike owner, but what bike should the budding shed builder choose? Unless it is all about the tech spec, go for simplicity and aesthetics – within reason. If you want to head off regularly to the coast at the weekend, or take that long-awaited European trip, there is no point buying a sweet little 125. Air-cooled engines are the easiest to work with, and it is always a benefit to have an engine that looks good. Some very

This barn find – a little stroker – could be exactly what the fledgling shed builder needs to begin. There is a dream bike somewhere for everyone in grub form, waiting to be discovered and worked on.

A shop-bought economy bike, bristling with potential for the initiate, is halfway there. The experience of cleaning it up and carrying out some mild customizing will be a solid stepping stone to more challenging projects.

lovely designed bikes are spoilt by using a pug-ugly lump, which would be best covered by a bonnet. You might want to avoid later fuel-injected models, unless you are not put off by the electronic control side (carbs can be good for you!).

For a first bike, a single is the most sensible consideration. There are some cute little customs using small engines of about 125cc, but, to be honest, unless you are limited to this size by licence, your money might be better spent on a pushbike and some steroids. A small-displacement bike can be made to go fast but, as it will have no grunt, everything becomes a bit too frenetic; it is difficult for a grown-up to look cool when thrashing the guts out of a little pumped-up moped. Get some practice on one by all means, but think how much more fun a bit more oomph could provide. Something with a bit of poke, such as a 250, should really be the bottom limit. The common choice will be a four-stroke, although there are plenty of older two-stroke machines around as well.

WHICH MODEL?

There is a staggering range of bike models around, so it is not really possible to discuss them all here; the following is a guide to the main engine types, covering the bikes in each configuration that suit a particular type for the lover of classic wheels. It is all very subjective – after all, everybody has a favourite bike that they really do not like. Obviously, the ones that are not mentioned can be a possible option, but their omission could be due to a reputation, an ugliness that cannot be rectified, or because they are just too embarrassing even to consider.

One Pot

Honda singles range from 125 up to 600. They are pretty tough machines and tend to go on for ever. The Yamahas are the same, the most popular being the SR and XT models. Most of these will provide a practical base bike to start with. (There are other oriental marques that have put out some nice bikes worth considering, but this guide will be kept concise and biased for the time being.) The long-stroke lump used in the Yamaha XT/TT/SR500 is probably the loveliest engine to use and, with a simple frame containing the oil, a doddle to tweak simply or to go the whole tuning hog. It is not very long-legged or top-end fast, but great for trackers, scramblers, supermoto or brat. The design is based on the old BSA singles, which, with some engine work, can turn a clean pair of heels around the corners, so a café racer is also an option. Parts are widely available and they are easy to work on and tune up.

XL/XR Hondas are all of the above but somehow do not look quite as sweet. In addition, a few have twin pipes, which adds to the complexity of customizing. However, they are Hondas, so they will repay your effort.

There are various single Brit bikes – AJS, Norton, Velocette – but flavour of the month are currently the Royal Enfield Bullet 350 or 500 singles, built in India and widely used for custom bikes. The results can look very nice, but old prejudices tend to die hard, and for many of my generation the concept (not the result) will always be treated with disparagement.

Twin Power

Before the rise in concerns over emissions and climate change, there were some cracking air-cooled two-stroke bikes. These can create lovely raw bikes, which may scare those used to the placid singles and twins of the same period. Yamaha were the leaders in this, with their reed-valve two-stroke engines powering some serious bikes; for a road-sensible bike, go for the DT250/360/400. Enduro and scramblers used pokier engines and these are also good fun; keep an eye out for Husqvarna, Honda, Maico, Bultaco, Suzuki strokers as a good starting point for something different.

ABOVE: *A pair of mid-range Honda fours in a sorry state would be an ideal purchase – all the necessary parts are there, enough probably to make one good bike and with some left over to trade, sell or keep on the shelf. The distinctive Comstar wheels are getting rarer, while undented classic tanks are money in the bank.*
LEFT: *The Ducati Desmo single (named for the type of valve-actuating mechanism) is rare and expensive – and gorgeous. It is a perfect prospect for a simple clean custom, although it can be a bit temperamental to own. A good grasp of mechanics is required to keep this bike and similar beauties on the road.*

Twins come in a variety of configurations, including verticals, as in Triumphs and other Brit bikes, all the usual Jap players and some rare breeds. V-twins come from Harleys, Moto Guzzi, Ducati and now quite a few Japanese manufacturers. The flat twins are dominated by BMW, although Dnieper and some East European models can also be considered.

Triumph twins of the first period – Bonneville, T120 and so on – are very popular. It is easy to get parts for them and to work on them, and they have been custom sleds since the year dot, widely used as the base motors for café racers and chops. They also have an impressive flat-track and off-road heritage, and have become some of the most recognizable bikes in the world. Relatively small and light, they will slot into many other frames and also feature a pretty-looking lump.

The Norton Commando has possibly one of the best-looking engines and can work in a wide range of styles, from flat-tracker to full-on chop (although some might consider it a sacrilege to waste such an exquisite motor in this way). They are also pre-unit – the gearbox is separate from the engine, as on Harleys that are not Sportsters – making them trickier to drop into alternative frames.

The Japanese 'Bonnie', the XS650, is widely used in trackers and street chops. Good-looking, readily tunable with easily available parts and very reliable, this is probably the best midrange beast around. Kawasaki also have a new version of the upright twin out, which is being used by many trendy bike-builders.

The new Bonneville, lauded as the epitome of the retro trend in bikes, comes in many guises. Sadly, Triumph's version is a bland, tubby little bike without any of the slender beauty of the original Bonnies, or the performance of modern bikes, but the company's marketing has been spectacular, so it is very popular and selling well. Second-hand versions are now coming on to the market and, as the model is used for nearly all the new hip customs, there is plenty of aftermarket stuff available to turn it into a dream machine – hopefully without involving a brown slab of a seat, coddled pipes and petite indicators.

Built to take the worst, this XT500 had been stashed outside a garage for many years. Pulled from a snowdrift, sprayed with WD and fuelled, it started up successfully; cash changed hands and another addition to the stable had been procured.

Tough as nails, this XS650 was bought online in Florida and ridden by me 3,000 miles back to west Canada. Knowing the bike, I was able to sort out the inevitable mishaps (breakdowns, if you must) using carried tools and ingenuity. Building and riding shed-built bikes is always an enjoyable and satisfying adventure, and you do meet the nicest people.

There are many other British and Japanese vertical twins from the early days up to now, most of which are solid and dependable, although without the options for tuning and rebuilding enjoyed by those described above. Some are rare, so it is vital to check that this rarity is not down to the bike having been a useless dog (Norton Jubilee and Honda Dream, to name but two), and remember that parts can be pricy or hard to find.

Obviously, the V-twin of choice for customizing has for some time been the Harley. The earlier ones are good-looking, easy to work on and have the largest range of optional extras – though most of these are in the shiny, heavy and crass

This Ironhead Sportster from the 1970s – named, like all Harleys, after the type of cylinder head – is still cool and a reasonable price. These bikes were made for customizing, and will never go down in value.

Jacques' nice mash-up of a BMW motor in a Dnieper frame and chair, with leading link forks that are sidecar favourites, small wheels, good disc brakes and little else needed. Solid and chunky, it is a practical workhorse for not a lot of money.

The old-school sports Honda was cutting edge when it came out and a bike to be reckoned with, all faired up and with big brakes.

league. Some of the early rolling gear is quite usable and early frames are useful, but the ugly kit they come with nowadays and the unreasonable increase in weight are a real turn-off. Unit construction Sportsters are the best bet. The simple (some say crude) design makes life so much easier and they can be used for every type of custom, whereas the big twins (as they are known) are more or less limited to use as chops or bobbers.

Other V-twins include Moto Guzzi, Ducati, Moto Morini and nowadays lots of Japanese; there are also the rare old bikes such as Vincent, Jap and old Indians. All can be turned into custom bikes if necessary, but they come with their own, very specific demands: complicated engineering for the Italians to look good, a lot of imagination for the Japs, and a considerable amount of money for the classics.

Flat twins have been around for a long time and the air-cooled BMWs are simple, handsome and reliable bikes that can be lovely-looking when done right, or horrid in the wrong hands. There are many of them about and they go on for ever. There is a strong loyalty to this particular brand and most owners of standard bikes feel that it is sacrilege to tamper with them. In fact, some consider that using anything without BMW stamped on it to be a capital offence.

A late-model Beemer can be a good basis for a bike but it can become complicated; as in most modern bikes, the design is so integrated and clever that it almost demands a degree in electronics and engineering to change the simplest thing. Like many media-savvy companies tapping the lucrative market for customizing, the BMW factory has given new bikes away to workshops for makeovers, with interesting results (*see* later).

There is another flat twin, a copy of the early Beemers, that has not developed many good reviews in Britain, but is used extensively in Eastern Europe as a go-anywhere beast. They used to be cheap and, if maintained (very) regularly, would be a good little ride, but poor-quality components and engineering make them an eccentric choice. I owned a customized one once and it was the most unreliable bike I have ever had, so my opinion may be slightly biased.

ABOVE: Nowadays, streetfighters are the tool of choice for the fast gang. As this beast shows, with its minimal frame and limited comfort, it is all about the speed.

RIGHT: An ideal candidate for some custom work, a Military Beezer (BSA) on its last legs at an auction. Buying a bike in this condition forces the builder to pull out all the stops and, apart from the engine and frame, which do need some work, the rest is down to personal choice.

Multi-Cylindered Bikes

Multi-cylindered bikes – commonly Japanese, apart from a couple of Italian marques – are a major part of the custom scene. The first BSA/Triumph triple, which was used in the Hurricane, was one of the loveliest 'custom' bikes ever to come out of a factory and Triumph have produced some blistering triples and fours over the recent years. These tend to be larger in capacity, with increasing levels of complexity, which has evolved as technology has progressed and regulations have changed. The earlier air-cooled fours, especially the CB Hondas, make very good customs and can be easily transformed from mundane to masterly, with good-looking engines and simple components.

BUYING THE BIKE

Obviously there are exceptions to be had everywhere, so it is best to narrow down the field if this book is not going to end up as thick and heavy as a typical chrome-filled custom parts catalogue. The project bikes covered in the book

17

The breaker's yard, where the customizer could acquire in just one enjoyable afternoon enough project essentials for a couple of years of shed building. Buying engines, frames and other main parts separately, rather than a complete bike, can be economical and productive; everything will need cleaning, revamping and painting anyway.

Norton is a classic marque and, while the older models are interesting, the Commandos are beautiful, ridable bikes that lend themselves to customizing and tweaking with ease. As with larger-capacity bikes of this era, they are slim, elegant and uncluttered, and require very little specialist skill to be turned into a usable custom.

are a single (TT500 Yamaha), a V-twin (1200 Sportster) and a flat twin (BMW R100RT). These were worked on while the book was being conceived and custom changes to these bikes will be used to lead into other areas..

Purchasing a used bike is always a risky business and in this situation it can be even worse. However, if you do want to make significant changes to your purchase, you may think it more pragmatic to buy that pig's ear, which you can then turn into a silk purse, rather than forking out loads for someone else's creation, only to spend time and money changing everything.

Try to visualize the extent to which you want to customize – is it going to be a full-blown effort with new frame and all rolling gear, or a cosmetic shunt, using mostly what is already there, with just a few mods? If it is just a makeover, then the donor bike will need to be pretty much up together and running well – preferably roadworthy – and all legal. Usually, when you have done your research and then made the effort to go and see a bike, the result will be that you buy it – unless there is a serious problem that puts you off. If you want that bike, recognize that everything can be fixed, and sometimes it is good to be impulsive and go with your heart, but do not forget: *caveat emptor…*

The Buying Process

When making buying decisions, you need not worry unduly about those items that wear out, such as chains, brakes and cables, as these are probably going to be on your to-do list immediately anyway. Unless you are absolutely certain, never ride around on a bike without being sure of the components that ensure safety and reliability. Hopefully, pointing out any worn items to the seller will get you a reduction in the price. Generally, vendors, whether private or trade, will already have allowed for concessions when setting their asking price, so do not be afraid to tyrekick and haggle. If you are uncertain, take along a friend who knows about these things and can support you, but always try to leave a deal without feeling done, and without feeling that you have harassed the vendor too much. They (and you) can always pull out at the last minute, but if you want it, buy it;

unless it is bent or a massive mechanical wreck, it can always be fixed.

If you fancy going the whole hog and building from the ground up, consider buying all the components separately, as this could save a lot of money and allow the project to come together as and when parts can be afforded or found. This approach could require a lot of legwork hunting for obscure parts if the bike is a rare one, so you need to weigh the purchase of a complete bike carefully against the cost, in terms of money and time, of acquiring all the bits piecemeal.

If you find something you like the look of, phone and get as much information as possible. Do not worry if the seller tells you that are other buyers interested; that is standard dealing bluff. Do some research: check forums for the bike for ideas on prices, issues and availability of parts; they are also good for discussing what can work, who sells it and how to fit it. If you intend to ride the bike when you go to view it, make sure the insurance is valid and that the bike is road-legal. Most vendors insist on holding the cash if the bike is being test ridden; take a photo of the vendor before you hand cash over, as it would be embarrassing to discover that they have let you ride off on a nicked bike and then done a runner themselves – it has happened!

When buying a bike, or big components for a bike, second-hand, always ask why they are being sold and make sure you are happy with the answer in terms of honesty. Stupidity should also be allowed for.

When viewing a bike to buy, ask the vendor to start it and you watch the routine; old bikes often have foibles that need to be indulged. When you are discussing a potential visit, ask them not to start the bike before you arrive, as cold starting might be harder than warm starting. Get the bike running, let it warm up, then turn it off for a couple of minutes and start again. It is possible to prep a dodgy bike to start and run for a couple of minutes in order to offload it and make it a new owner's problem.

The Legal Bits

Paperwork is an essential part of the task of buying a bike that is new to you. The safest way can be to purchase from an established dealer or a friend so you know that everything is above board, but there are checks you can do to ensure that all is in order. The engine and frame numbers (VIN) should match up and should also be the same in the registration documents. If they do not, you should be suspicious and back off; such discrepancies will not stop the work on the bike, but they can cause all sorts of problems when dealing with the law, or if an accident occurs. If you are really keen on a bike, check all the documents first, before you look at it in any detail. Glib explanations for dodgy paperwork can sound more plausible the more you want a bike, so you must be sensible. The best-case scenario is that the bike is made up of any old rubbish and may die any minute, the worst is that it is stolen and, if you are stopped by the law, it will be impounded, with no chance of compensation.

Checking Things Over

If it is legit and you still want it, everything then needs to be checked. If it is being bought as a project, go through the stuff below in the components, but if you mean to ride it straight away, make sure everything works, it goes okay and that it stops. This is a minefield for the inexperienced so, if you are unsure about what to look for, and the pressure of being observed pulling

Purchased from a police auction, this stolen and recovered Sportster engine has had a mild going-over to make it a bit more special than standard. The push-rod tubes have been turned on a small lathe, while the case bolts have been set into counterbores. The contrasting polish and paint makes it clean and tidy.

The product of a bored farm mechanic, this quad was seen in passing and, after a quick haggle, bought cheap. Throwing away the weird stuff resulted in a perfectly usable frame, engine and some rolling parts, creating the perfect base for a project.

of abuse. Check the spark plugs for excess carbon build-up or whiteout. Compression can be checked with a tester to see if it is within stated guidelines (or ask a garage or a mate what it should be). If the sprocket is excessively worn or there are worn splines on gear-change shafts, it can indicate a thrashed and poorly maintained bike. Look for gasket goo on joints and chewed-up fasteners, which could be the result of a rough rebuild. Take the oil filter and/or the drain plug out and look for any unwanted chunks of metal that have come off the internals. Put a gear lever on and turn the sprocket to check if all the gears can be engaged. If the splines are worn down (but not an issue), use a mole grip attached to the shaft to select the gears.

An engine from a bike that has been written off can be a good buy, as the reason for selling is not usually mechanical failure. On the other hand, it may have a scuffed or broken casing.

Never buy an engine that has numbers (VIN) that are not on the place where they should be. Each factory uses a specific style and letterform and there may also be indent hatching to prevent them being removed and replaced. Check that this is the correct one.

someone's bike to pieces is likely to be a distraction, take a friend who knows. Old bikes rattle, have oil in unexpected places and can seem, if you are used to modern bikes, to be low on power, with

scarily inefficient brakes and weird idiosyncrasies in starting or riding.

For a big purchase, ask to meet the seller at a garage. For a small cost (which you might be able to recoup in negotiating a lowered price), have it checked over by a mechanic. Never buy a bike unseen, as this can lead to much disappointment or stress.

The Engine
Try not to buy a partial engine, as the missing parts are invariably the costliest bits, and can ramp up the cost of the rebuild. Conversely, a complete engine is always going to be an unknown factor, so give it a good look over for signs

The Frame
Frames come with a VIN that should be matched to the legal documents of the bike (and hopefully the engine), so check for this and ask to see the registration papers. These should come as part of the deal, unless it is a custom-made

Damaged splines on the gear lever had been bodged on, then a weld added, which failed somewhere out in the wilds, losing the gear lever. It needed a lot of work to get back on the road.

clean hands

When rooting through old bikes with a view to buying one, carry a small bottle of hand cleaner and some paper roll for a quick clean-up. At home, it is a good idea to keep a big tub of industrial hand-cleaning gel. Alternatively, a mixture of cooking oil and sugar can be used to clean garage hands.

Standard frames are fairly cluttered with brackets and mounts, but, apart from accident damage, not a lot goes wrong with them and they are often quite cheap to buy.

frame, for which you will want a bill of sale and serial number. You will need this to make life easier when doing the paperwork to get it road-legal. Check the condition of the motor mounts; take a collection of bolts to slide through these and then eye them up. Look for kinks in the tubes and check all is true and square. Even the smallest deviation can affect handling and, at high speed, turn a bike into a death trap. Do not forget to make sure that it is the correct frame for the engine, or, if an alternative, that the engine will fit in and there is clearance for the exhaust and carbs. Is the swing arm coming with it and, if so, has it got the spindle? These are not cheap and they can be prone to corrosion with seized bearings locked on them.

Forks have one real purpose and that is to provide even and progressive suspension, so they must move up and down smoothly without catching. Take each leg and press the tube into the slider; they should be equal in resistance. Do not worry about oil on the legs from leaking seals; look for scoring where they go into the slider. Check the condition of the chrome around the seals and the exposed part in the yokes for pitting. In the past, it was common practice to wire-brush this out and fill with resin before polishing back to the surface – it might be an extreme remedy but, if the parts are rare, it may be necessary.

Are the yokes (or triple tree) included? Is the steering-head spindle in good condition? Check the condition of the thread. If this is the type for the frame but the yokes are to be changed, can the spindle be removed? It will be expensive to get one machined up.

Every discovery will need to be given the once-over. On this lovely old enduro, the tops of the stanchions were rusty, so new ones would be needed. There was no spark plug, so water may have got inside and seized the engine, necessitating a comprehensive (and expensive) rebuild. All other parts looked to be in good condition, considering its age and location.

A modern Ducati given the classic racer treatment at Redmax Speed Shop. The bike needed very little tweaking, but was enhanced by some lovely bodywork, a stylish paint job and Peashooter silencers.

If a spindle is seized in the hub or brake plate, spray liberally with WD40 and leave to soak, then warm up the surrounding metal and drive out with a soft-headed mallet or a block of wood and a hammer.

Bead breaker: to break the bead on a tyre; use clamps to squeeze the tyre walls together.

LEFT: *A definite rat bike: it runs, is road-legal and even comes with its own shed. Is it the perfect project?*

Wheels

Cast-alloy wheels will tend to fracture in a shunt, so give them a good inspection for rim integrity and the condition of the valve hole. Use a bolt to check that all the threads in the hub are sound and look at the bearings for a good fit in the hub. If they are not in, check that the seat is not oval with a vernier.

Wire-spoked wheels should be checked for loose or bent spokes, and the state of the nipples looked at for excess corrosion that will prevent reuse or adjustment. Check the hub as above.

Out-of-true rims can be identified by putting them in a spindle clamped to a bench (or similar), then spinning it while holding a stick or screwdriver to the rim. If it wobbles, moves away or rubs, then it will need repair work or to be rejected. Dings and scuffs in alloy rims can be taken out by careful work. If the idea is to have rebuilt wheels, which is really the best way if any polishing or painting is to be done, hubs and rims can be bought separately. Be aware that they are not designed on a universal template, so you will need to check that the number of spokes holes are the same and also that spoke angles line up from hub to rim. Buying a cheap hub might result in having to purchase an expensive rim to match, whereas a complete wheel can be stripped down, with only spokes having to be purchased.

If you buy a second-hand wheel, make sure you know what it is from, as finding brake pads or discs to fit can be an insurmountable task if you do not have the make and model info.

READY TO GO...

Once your collection of bits is in the shed, put it all together roughly, to start assessing what will be needed to turn the bike into a viable machine. Purchase a decent manual or download one from the internet, clear the workbenches and then get going.

3

workshop and tools

THE SHED

People who think or make often need a quiet space in which to accomplish their dreams. Creative activities usually demand a special place, be it a workshop, studio or a room or even a small corner in the house. Whatever it is in reality, this will henceforth be referred to as 'the shed', in honour of all the fantastic bikes that have come into being in a wooden hut at the end of the garden. The building of such a structure is a subject for another book, so, assuming that you are already in possession of such a place and have control over its decoration and fitting out, the following advice will help you create an idealized shed, and describe the lovely things that will help you build your bike.

be safe

The point of building bikes is to enjoy them and for that you will need to have all the physical bits that you started with present and working properly. Look after yourself! Always be aware of the hazards and risks involved in using tools, especially power tools, and in hefting heavy parts or complete bikes about. Read any technical bumf that comes with any kit and do not neglect any safety instructions. If you are using online resources for hazardous work instructions, it is always cross-referencing with other sources. One very popular and influential site advising on disc cutters only mentions in passing that 'safety glasses might be handy'.

Safety and Security

Before you start any work, stand back and consider the tasks before you, what you will use to complete them and how you can prevent damage or injury. Next, figure out what you can do if and when issues or problems arrive. Take a tip from the scouts: be prepared.

A respectable workshop with the basic amenities: good light, storage space and room to walk around the bike. Anything more is helpful, but good customizing is still possible with these simple facilities.

Access

It is useful to be able to wheel the bike in and out, and a non-slip path and ramp will be indispensable for this. It will need to be non-slip, as pushing a partially built bike with no brakes around can be a hazardous business. Inside, the more space you have the better. You can only run with what you have got, but try to have enough room to walk around the bike as it is assembled. Working on a side bench is fine for engines and components, but awkward for something a couple of metres long and ungainly to boot.

Light

A gloomy ambience may look great in an ad, but it is not suited to working. Install some cheap but efficient neon lights, so that you do not have to squint at the work, which might cause premature wrinkles around your eyes. Dedicated lights for illuminating work on lathes and drills will increase output and accuracy, and reduce the risk of accidents.

Air

It is essential to have decent ventilation for most work, from spray painting to grinding and polishing. If you are

23

Part of my shanty town of sheds that has evolved over the years. Big doors allow lots of light and access and it is pleasant to work outside. The floor is made of reclaimed scaffold planks that can take a lot of punishment. The shelving and storage have been sourced cheaply or for free from skips and boot sales, so, if better units turn up, there is no reason to keep them.

A boxed-off area for the anti-social work such as painting and using the blast cabinet. The latter is a useful contraption that pays for itself in time saved cleaning metal and in being able to do the job right away.

carrying out a lot of this type of work, you may need to get an extraction unit of some sort to reduce the particles being breathed in, and to prevent everything being coated with dust. Rubbing, grinding or polishing with machines will cause your hands and the surfaces around you to be covered in grime. This is because they produce fine airborne dirt, composed of metal, oil and cleaning chemicals, and this travels easily around the work area. If you are not wearing a filter mask, or you cannot hold your breath for longer than ten minutes, a lot of this muck will end up inside you.

In damper conditions, condensation can also be a pain if there is less than adequate draught-proofing.

Locking Up

Get a good-quality hasp for the main door and use a solid padlock. Inside, if there are more bikes, set floor anchors in and use a good chain to secure bikes to them.

The Bench

After an adolescence spent wrenching in a corner of the family garage, with the subject usually on the ground, I discovered benches. They have made an amazing contribution to my quality of life. If you are going to work on motorbikes for any length of time it is worth investing in a lifting bench that allows the bike to come up to a decent working height, for access to all parts. These are not that expensive in the most basic form – mine was bought at an autojumble for less money than it would cost to acquire the metal to make one from scratch, and will outlast my working life.

A sturdy homemade bike bench will do if necessary; it does not need to be full height as any elevation will be useful. Try to build in a ramp, or a ramp attachment, so the bike can be wheeled up or down. Be aware that, as the bike gets higher while it is being pushed up a ramp, it becomes harder to control and could topple over. A step will help, as will a working front brake to hold it in place while you readjust your position. When putting a bike on a bench, have all the blocks and stands for holding the bike upright ready at hand; preferably have a friend to help, in case the bike tips over. The same goes for getting down a finished bike with fragile parts and new paint.

Side benches are great for doing all the little jobs. Good solid surfaces for these can be created from reject kitchen tops, usually found in skips on building sites.

Shelving and Storage

Places to pack away all the spare bits of bike, bigger tools and cans will always be needed. Do not get too precious about this; start off using whatever is at hand or found, then, as time passes, the perfect shelving unit or cupboard will materialize. Make sure they are sturdy and level.

TOOLS ON THE BENCH

Bench Grinder

The bench grinder is a basic workhorse for shaping metal, sharpening drill bits and numerous other tasks. Get the best you can afford, along with, if possible, a selection of wheels, including polishing and buffing wheels. Mount it securely, as it will shake any loose fitting to bits, and have a can with water for quenching hot metal screwed to the wall next to it. Keep the rests and guards in good condition and securely fixed; you might want to consider taking off and refitting all the bolts using Loctite.

Pillar Drill

Making holes in metal is a big part of custom work and, while a hand electric drill is fine, a solid bench-mounted drill will make your life easier, and your work much more accurate. Check out machinery sales for good-quality second-hand machines – you could pick one up for less than the price of a new, high-quality hand drill. Do not be put off by grime and surface rust on a second-hand item. As long as there is no play in the bearings – and this is easily fixed anyway – it should suffice.

Lathe

A lathe is an incredibly useful piece of machinery to have, for turning up spacers, boring accurate holes and bearing surfaces, cleaning the ends of cut rod and bolts and giving fancy finishes to many components. They range from little model-maker's machines to great industrial beasts, so the choice is wide. You may be able to get hold of an old lathe from a small workshop for a reasonable price. These are almost antiques, but, owing to the quality of their construction, will outlast many of the lightweight contemporary ones that are pumped out today using cheap materials and weak motors. It is a sad fact that the older generation of shed users are dying off and that many do not have an heir to carry on their passion; the one silver lining of this cloud is that they tended to have solid dependable kit, purchased before the markets were flooded with cheap, disposable 'tools', and this equipment often ends up on the market. My own lathe is over 60 years old and with routine maintenance will easily last that again. Do some research and, if you have the funds and the space, get one!

learning

Check whether there are any evening classes in metalwork, machining or similar in your area. It is a good way to learn the basics and practise with skilled tutors who, if they become interested in your project, could provide other services such as welding or milling.

This project is held upright on a bench by using a small wind-up extending bike stand. Blocks will do the same job, but will require a friend to help with lifting. The ratchet straps prevent the bike tipping or rolling.

Pillar drill or drill press.

Bargain lathe, which was found lurking under a seller's table at an autojumble. It was acquired for less cash than a second-hand tyre and carried triumphantly home.

Compressor

Compressors often come up on the second-hand market. Look for a well-maintained one, preferably with a blowgun, tyre-pump head and spray gun. A cheap one is fine for general use, but it is unlikely to be able to keep up the pressure for air tools or paint spraying. Keep your compressor oiled and clean.

POWER AND POWER TOOLS

If the shed has electric sockets, make sure they are easily accessible. Mount them above the back of workbenches and near to the machines. Have a dedicated extension lead with a power trip and waterproof socket that can reach outside. Keep spare fuses handy for when the power is overloaded, or a tool has been worked too hard.

Every tool has its rules and a set of precautions that apply to it. In the case of power tools, many of these are the same for each tool every time. Learn these by heart and you will always be off to a safe start:

- Always read, understand and follow the instruction manual before attempting to use any power tool in any way. Also read the nameplate

Working with power tools is not to be taken lightly. The image of sparks flying in a darkened garage may be pretty, but when it goes wrong bad things can happen.

Most shed builders and mechanics have done this in their time, but failure to use the correct guards etc. is wrong and dangerous. Do not get into the habit of risky practices; it may seem fine until the one time when it is not.

information and follow the warning labels on the tool itself.

- Always wear safety goggles or safety glasses with side shields.
- Use a dust mask for dusty operations, and wear hearing protection if you will be using the tool for an extended period of time.
- Dress correctly: no loose-fitting clothing, no neckties, no jewellery, no dangling objects of any kind. Long hair must be tied back out of your way.
- Safety footwear must be worn and laces tied.
- Make sure your work area is neat and clean and free of any debris that might get in your way or could be ignited by hot tools, chips or sparks.
- Make sure your work area is well illuminated and that there is adequate ventilation, to prevent the build-up of dust that could obscure work.
- Ensure that the machine is not damaged, cables are clean of cuts and that plugs are attached correctly. All machinery bought second-hand from a dealer should have a current Portable Appliance Test (PAT) certificate.
- Before you plug in any power tool, make sure the power switch is off.
- Be sure all appropriate guards are in place, secure and working.
- Always turn off and unplug the tool before you make any adjustments or change accessories.
- Allow the machine to come to a stop by its own volition – do not jam it into the bench or floor, for example, to slow it down.
- Always use the correct spanners/keys for changing and tightening blades and bits.
- Never use any accessory except those specifically supplied or recommended by the manufacturer. They should be described in the tool's instruction manual.
- Never use power tools in wet or damp conditions.
- Never use a tool that is damaged or malfunctioning in any way.
- Need an extension cord? Make sure it is a heavy-duty one and do not use 24V cords outside without a cut-out unit and a waterproof, covered socket.
- Never use power tools if you are tired, sick, distracted, or under the influence of drugs or alcohol.
- Make sure cutters or blades are clean, sharp and securely in place. Never use bent, broken or warped blades or cutters.
- Use the correct blade for the material you are cutting.
- Ensure that the material to be cut is secure and cutting will not damage other material. Do not use hands or feet to hold material in position.
- Never overreach when using a power tool. Stay firmly planted on both feet.
- Never rush what you are doing. Always pay close attention. Do not let anything distract you. Think ahead!
- When using hand-held power tools, always keep a firm grip with both hands. Losing control creates a hazardous situation. Do not use any tool that is too heavy for you to control easily.
- Always use the right tool for the right job. No substitutions allowed!
- Always unplug, clean and store the tool in a safe, dry place when you have finished using it.

ODDS AND ENDS

For a productive shed, there are certain items and sundries that should be included in the roll call. Adding to the following list is mandatory.

- Fire extinguisher(s); powder or CO_2, never water.
- Waste bin; big, tough plastic tubs are best, kept away from the workbench. It is a pain when something is dropped to have to empty the bin looking for it.
- Rags and hand towel; old T-shirts, sheets and cotton items, cut up ready for use. Rolls of industrial paper towel, hung on an old towel rail for ease of access.
- First aid box, for immediate treatment of cuts and bits in eyes; hand sanitizer, plasters, eyewash and some disposable gloves.
- Box of disposable gloves; saves having to dive indoors constantly

Having a sturdy engineering vice is similar to having a spare pair of hands and life in the shed is difficult without one. Make up jaw covers from aluminium sheet or angle bar to prevent marks on softer metals.

and wash hands when handling oil and grease. Also good for first aid moments, but keep separate from the ones from the first aid kit.

- Blocks of wood (offcuts), for support and packing.
- Tape; gaffer, masking and insulation. If the shed is prone to damp, keep them in a lidded plastic container with silica gel.
- Lubricants and cleaners; WD40, grease, copper grease, carb cleaner, degreaser.
- Loctite and Studlok; one of each will last for years.
- Wire wool and emery cloth.
- Cutting lubricant; keep secure by lathe or drill. You can buy the concentrate to make it up.
- Bag of sawdust, cat litter or fine sand, in a handy spot, ready to soak up spills.
- Carpet squares for putting painted or polished items on to prevent damage; scrounge a sample book from a shop – they throw them away regularly.
- Plastic trays or boxes with compartments; store nuts, bolts and washers in separate sets. Have them also for electrical components, O-rings, clips, and so on.
- Old vacuum cleaner; the amount of dust generated in a shed is going to coat everything in a layer of grime, get a large paintbrush and dust off into the vacuum's hose when cleaning up.
- Straps; ratchet or locking straps for securing the bike on the bench or in a trailer.
- Small jack; useful to lift up the engine or bike slightly, to fit parts or set up on blocks.

BASIC KIT OF HAND TOOLS

Without tools the human race would be still living in damp caves, getting generally fed up with things – think how much worse it would be if you wanted to build bikes in these conditions. Luckily for gearheads, but not necessarily for the planet, boredom is the mother of invention, and we now benefit from a vast range of tools and equipment that can improve our lives. The most important of these inventions was obviously the wheel; surely, it was the realization that two of

Good solid bench grinder and behind it a plenisher, set up in the 'dirty' room to minimize dust and mess. The murky cylinder at the bottom is actually a red fire extinguisher.

these could be the basis for a bike that marked the birth of civilization.

If you want to carry out work on a bike, then the acquisition of tools will be an absolute necessity. Once your collection has been started, it will never be finished. Gearheads come to love tools and will always find reasons to buy more, knowing that a well-stocked toolkit is one of the main ingredients of happiness.

Starting a Toolkit

The range of tools required for the majority of stripping and building is surprisingly small if looked at logically.

The average bike is manufactured with as few variations in size of fasteners as possible, to keep costs down and make assembly easier. The main difference in the overall number of tools necessary will be the type of bike and probably its age; old British and American will use imperial measurements, while everything else will be metric, so if you are going to work on both types you will need two sets of tools.

It is easy to go shopping and buy a 'comprehensive' toolkit all wrapped up in one tidy plastic case. Unfortunately, these are generally churned out of factories under nameless brands, using the cheapest materials and subject to

Cut a plastic container in half to make a degreasing bath, making sure it is supported level. If it does not have a ledge, like this bottle, put in a mesh stand to rest the component on.

information

The workshop manual for the bike, or engine, will be absolutely fundamental to the project. If you have moved past mere paper, you should be able to download it on to a tablet or laptop, although in my experience it takes no time at all to render touch-screens and keyboards filthy and unusable. Perhaps some people have a better grasp of shed hygiene…

TOP RIGHT: *Spanners (left to right): socket spanners from France; combination with ratchet; combination with swivel-head ratchet; combination; open-ended; OEM tool-roll spanners; short combination; ring spanner.*
RIGHT: *This metal filing drawer cabinet was discarded in an office clear-out. Sturdy and compact, it is ideal for storing most of the hand tools needed in a shed. Find similar items on online auction sites or at the local scrapyard – just do not let the kids label it.*

little quality control. They can also be picked up at second-hand shops or boot sales for very little. The tendency, however, is to relegate the majority of the items to the back of the shed, keeping and using just the one tool in the set that actually works well. Even the better-quality kits, which can get very expensive, will often yield only a couple of regularly used tools, while the rest gather dust and decrease in value.

Starting from scratch is always difficult, and looking at somebody's well-stocked bike shed with an established and comprehensive toolkit, it could seem an expensive and intimidating task. (Be aware, too, that an owner who adorns his walls with his spanners and other stuff probably does not use them that often – unless he is hyper-tidy. Tools that are used often are usually kept close to hand in drawers or chests, or scattered across the workbench.) Hopefully, you will soon become acquainted with other bike owners who can give you friendly advice, but it is a good idea to start with a small range of high-end, quality tools that cover most aspects of the work. As the situation demands, you can then buy more individually, lessening the burden on your wallet.

The commonest fasteners used to hold a bike together are M10, M8 and M6, so you will need six spanners (to hold each end) and three Allen keys. Add to this two of each screwdriver type, a spark-plug socket, axle-nut spanners, pliers and mole grips. The result will be a toolkit that should cover most of the work needed to swap things out and keep a bike running, but this is not the whole story and more tools will always be necessary.

The following is a rundown of what to have in a decent start-up toolkit.

Spanners

A spanner is used to undo or tighten the hexagonal head on a bolt or a nut when a socket cannot get in, or for setting up. They are designated by the size of the nut they fit. Usually in chromium steel, the difference in price between poor and better quality is not really that significant. Go with a good brand that offers a good guarantee – usually lifetime – and, as with all tools, compare the finish and working surface quality. One set of combination spanners (open-end and ring-end) should be enough when coupled with a socket set, covering 99 per cent of all the nut sizes used on a bike. For the menial

task of holding the odd nut, a cheaper set can be purchased. When you need a specific size that is not in the set, buy it singly. At autojumbles and second-hand markets, start collecting any variations, but always with a mind to quality.

Ratchet spanners have a one-way mechanism that allows them to turn continuously from back and forth levering. They are very handy, but slightly limited in terms of where they can access and still be useful. For better access and control, a socket set will be needed.

Sockets

Basically, the socket is a steel tube that fits on to a nut at one end and has a square hole for the ratchet drive in the other. They come in various lengths so that they can cope with different depths of recessed nuts. The ratchet handle, made to turn one way, can be reversed, converting lever action to a continuous rotation. For awkward places, extension bars and flexible knuckle joints are used between the ratchet and the socket. Buy a good set with a range from 7mm up, with extension tools. Ensure that you have a socket for any spindle nuts, as spanners do

not really do the job well enough to be safe.

The square drive lugs of a ratchet come in quarter-inch, three-eighths and half-inch sizes. The best all-round size for the home workshop is three-eighths, while the larger half-inch is the one used in business. Preferred for sizes over 18mm and engine mount bolts, the half-inch can also be used with compressed-air ratchet guns; they are impressive to use but only with a decent compressor. Air guns can also work impact sockets, which are dark grey and chunkier than chrome standard ones; they impart a sudden force to a nut and will loosen a really tight one. They are not always necessary in the shed but it is useful to know someone who has one.

Torque Wrench

The fasteners on a bike need specific tensions and the torque wrench is used to impart a measured amount of force when tightening. When it is set to the torque needed, it makes a noise or slips when tight. You should only need to buy one of these. Get the best and make sure the drive is the same as your sockets. When not in use, wind it back down to the zero setting.

Socket kit with extension bars and knuckle joints (left); sockets including two box spanners for plugs, centre and ratchets (below); air socket gun (right) and torque wrench (bottom).

Getting leverage on stiff Allen bolts: If the bolt is so recessed you have to use the long section of the Allen key to get to it, and find there is not enough leverage to undo it, slip a ring spanner over the end and use that for extra torque.

Tee-handle Allen key set in a handy rack will cover all socket-head bolts on a bike. You can pick up single ones for pennies at boot sales and autojumbles; carry a bit of wire wool to clean the shaft and check the size.

Allen Keys

Used on socket-head (Allen) bolts, the basic Allen key is a bent piece of hex bar. The better versions have a longer shaft and are chamfered at the long end to allow use at an angle; this is very handy for getting into awkward spots and the long shaft helps for deep-set bolts. Even better are the 'T'-handled versions, with a long shaft and an angled head. All varieties come in sets, which include sizes that you may never find a use for. Be aware that, as they can be imperial or metric, some will seem to fit, but may not. If it is not a perfect fit in the socket, you risk rounding the inside and ending up with the bolt stuck without any grip. You will then need to use an extractor or to weld a nut on to get it out.

Screwdrivers

Many production bikes used to have engine covers fastened with a screw-driver-head bolt (or machine screws). These would be useless after chewing up the edges a couple of times, which is why it is a good idea to change them all out for Allen bolts. There are still many things on a bike that need a screwdriver, usually a Phillips (cross-head) version. These are often made out of softer metal than normal, so look for a range of decent hardened-tip screwdrivers to handle all sizes. Do

tapping new threads

Tips for threading (tapping) holes to take bolts or studs: first, drill a hole using a bit of the correct size; refer to the available tables to find the correct drill to use, or use the basic formula TD = MD − TP, where TD is the (tap) drill size, MD is the outer (major) diameter of the bolt (for example, M10x1.5 is 10mm) and TP is the thread pitch. So if TD = 10 − 1.5, use an 8.5mm bit, giving a 75 per cent thread. The taps are sequential: tapered for the first run through, intermediate and then bottom or plug for the final run, or to go in a blind hole. Use cutting compound and feed in the tap with a tap wrench a turn or so at a time, often backing out half a turn to remove the material into the groove.

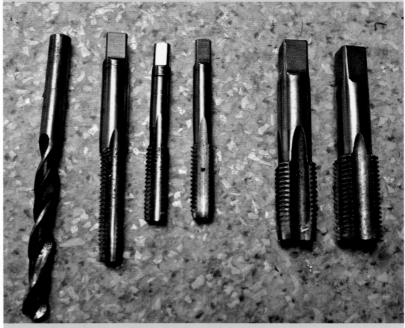

Taps are another essential in the shed toolkit.

Useful tools hanging up: hammers and hacksaws surround a bank of electric sockets and gauges from the compressor stationed outside.

An autojumble is an excellent source of cheap, often high-quality tools. Put a list of the sizes and types that you need on to your phone for quick reference when a buffet like this is found.

not buy carpentry ones, as these will chew up the screw head.

Flat-blade screwdrivers are used for electrical fittings and are good for hooking under circlips and flanges, which means they will invariably get bent out of shape. Once again, have a range to play with, or buy some cheap sacrificial ones.

The impact driver is used for getting stubborn screws and bolts out by imparting a fast, serious turning force when hit with a hammer. It is handy to have, especially if you are working on rusty 'barn-find' bikes.

Grippers

Pliers and mole grips are versatile tools for a wide range of tasks, often just for getting out of trouble. Pliers come in a variety of jaws, the essentials being long-nose, circlip and flat-nose. Check how well the jaws seat together, the quality of the pivot and always look for sensible rubber handles.

Mole grips have various types of jaw; the two to choose are flat parallel

and slightly curved. Cheapo ones will almost inevitably let you down.

Hammers

There is an abundance of hammers available, with heads for everything! Get a nice weighty engineer's hammer with a dome on one side and a circular flat on the other, sometimes called a ball-peen, and then buy other types as you come across them. Ideally, pick them up second-hand – handles are cheap to replace and heads do not tend to wear out. Look out for soft hammers that can be used to drive parts of a bike together without damaging the metal; the engineer's hammer and a block of wood is a good substitute.

Vernier Gauge

The best gauges are digital, as reading them does not rely on any skills. They are essential for the instant and exact sizing of bolts, spacers or anything else. On a bike project this is vital, especially when using non-standard parts.

ADDITIONAL HAND TOOLS

With the basic toolkit it should be possible to strip down a bike, swap out parts and maintain your machine. That is not the end of it, though, and there are many more tools that will be useful in the world of the custom builder. You can build up an impressive collection but be aware of the cost-to-use ratio and spend spare money on the bike first. Below is a quick overview of additional items, with their use and practicality.

Tyre Levers

Tyre levers are effective for old, tube-type tyres. There is a bit of a knack to using them correctly, but they are essential for long adventure rides. Pack with a puncture repair kit.

Adjustable Spanner or Wrench

Good for those times when a bolt needs holding while the other end is being worked on with the right spanner. Do not use for everyday fastening or undoing as they can round off heads too easily. Always rotate against the fixed jaw.

Tongue and Groove Pliers

Adjustable for grip and quick to use effectively, tongue and groove pliers are halfway between pliers and mole grips. They will get a lot of work and this can erode the pivot pin, allowing them to slip. Once this has happened, they should be binned.

Centre Punch

Never drill a hole without first centre-popping its exact position with a centre punch tool; at a pinch, you can use a sharp nail for a disposable substitute. The centre punch can also be used to tighten up loose rivets and drive stubs out.

Multimeter

Useful for checking new wiring systems or finding faults, a multimeter is not that expensive. A cheap version can be made using the battery, two lengths of wire and a bulb. For troubleshooting electrical systems and components, this is a must-have.

Feeler Gauge

Primarily for gauging gaps on plug and points, but it can also prove very useful when shimming or checking tolerances in engine-building or engineering.

C Spanner

For adjusting shocks and some securing rings. The cheap ones wear out after first use, so it is worth buying a better-quality version, with a hinged lock for improved grip.

Torx System

This is a star-shaped key for nuts with Torx recess, which are used increasingly by manufacturers for fasteners. The design prevents damage to the head of the bolt.

Steel Rule

For everything, really; get a short one and a long one.

Magnetic Dish

Perfect for keeping all those little bits tidy while working, although sadly not great for non-magnetic stainless-steel fasteners. It can also be handy if you need to check whether a bolt or part is mild or stainless.

Inspection Light

A standard garage tool, essential for throwing some light into all those dark corners and underneath work. It needs a hook or clamp for positioning and a power switch at the light end to be useful.

Tyre-Pressure Gauge

Tyre pressure should be checked weekly.

Hand Files

For all fine finishing and truing up, hand files come in a range of profiles. Buy them as needed and build up a selection.

Combination Square

For the setting out of holes, and for finding heights and depths.

Jigsaw

For making templates out of hardboard and wood, and for cutting GRP and thin metal sheet. You will need to have a selection of suitable blades.

Hacksaw

A hacksaw is cheap to buy, so have a couple at least, fitted with different blades – coarse for aluminium and fine for harder metals. The important point is the quality of the blade; those cheap bundles on sale at the market will wear out faster than a chocolate tyre.

Clamps

You will need G clamps for engineering stuff and quick- or trigger-action for holding pieces together and securing metal in place for working on. Old solid clamps can often be found for sale second-hand; make sure they wind up properly and any rust on the threads is only on the surface.

Snips

Snips, either straight or curved, are used for cutting sheet metal and wire; check the build quality as they are put under a lot of stress. A bench-mounted sheet cutter that makes light work of straight cuts is always a good purchase.

Drill

Modern cordless drills and drivers are tough and useful, but a good one will be relatively costly. If you can find an old-school mains drill second-hand, it will be a fraction of the price and is the one to have in the workshop. Do not buy the old-style key chucks, as they wear out and the keys tend to get lost. If it is all you have, attach the key with a length of wire or cable tie.

Level and Straight-Edge

These will be essential for setting up frames, aligning wheels and sprockets, and so on.

Tape Measure

Just have one, or two.

Engineer's Vice

The engineer's vice is an essential workshop item that will pay for itself very quickly. Get a good solid one with an anvil flat to allow you to beat out metal. A drill vice is a portable version that holds items to be drilled or welded wherever needed.

Torch

As an alternative to the inspection light, get a rechargeable one as batteries always run out at the wrong moment. A homemade version can have a 12V bulb in and wires with crocodile clips, to run off the bike power and keep for travelling.

Cold Chisel

Found at autojumbles and boot sales, a cold chisel can be used for the more violent tasks. A fine, sharpened one is great for knocking off weld spatter in tight places.

Multi-Bit Screwdriver

Handy for carrying about, but not a tool to rely on unless it is of the best quality.

Crowbar/Prybar

Put protective tape over the end and use it for levering engines up, pushing things into line or lifting whilst wedging up.

Utility Knife

Usually called a Stanley knife, this is essential for so many tasks. Buy a pack of good-quality blades, as it is easy to end up tearing material to pieces with a blunt edge.

STORAGE AND CARE

In the perfect hipster workshop all the tools are hung up on cool-looking boards, almost as if they're for show rather than use. But go to a busy workshop where work is actually carried out: the tool boards will be there, but supporting items that are rarely used, covered in dust. The everyday tools will be kept to hand on the benches, where they can be quickly scooped up, and stored in tool chests rather than painstakingly hung up in the correct spot on the wall.

So unless you hanker for this vision of a time gone past when life was leisurely and the apprentice would tidy up every evening, get real and get some storage drawers. Tool chests with drawers and cupboards should be a once in a lifetime purchase, so get the best you can, plus maybe solid boxes to bundle all of one type of tool together. My budget versions are steel filing cabinet, with shallow drawers, bought second-hand and very sturdy; one drawer holds all sockets, another spanners, and so on.

Tidy

While having loose tools everywhere can become counterproductive, experience shows that this is reality, so don't fret over it. Have a regular tidy up session when things get too chaotic or tools disappear; you'll soon know where everything is and where you put things down.

While allowing a certain amount of disorganization in the workshop, it's still important to look after your tools. When the inevitable tidy-up comes around, have old rags at hand and clean oil or grime off the tools as they are put away. An old paintbrush or the airline can get rid of dust, and if a toll is rarely used then apply a light spray of WD on the bare surfaces to keep corrosion at bay. Start collecting the silica-gel packets that appear in packaging nowadays and put a couple in each tool drawer/box to keep humidity down, especially in a shed that may not be airtight or warm. Should a sheen of moisture coat everything metal on cold mornings, don't let it build up: dry it off and use WD liberally.

ON THE ROAD

Taking a home-built bike out for long trips often becomes a lesson in roadside

Engines are not designed to be freestanding and they are dangerous if they are allowed to roll around on the bench. Use some scrap metal and take the opportunity to practise your welding and fabricating skills by knocking up a motor stand.

mechanics, as this will be the time when vibration and a moment's inattention in the shed can cause things to fall off, break or short out. Extended running can throw the tuning into disarray as well, so be prepared. Make up a travelling toolkit, comprehensive enough to cover most problems, which can be attached to or carried securely on the bike. After working in the shed, you should know which tools you use most often; make a list and set them aside. Now consider whether you want to have to make this set up each time you go for a ride, or lose half of it when working in the shed? It is best to have a portable kit kept separately, as an addition to the shed-based one. Buy or make a tool roll that can hold all the tools neatly, which can double as a dry surface to work off; the best type is canvas. Leather may be funky, but it is less flexible, while the plastic ones tend to crack and tear.

The essentials for your on-the-road kit are:

- Three or four spanners; M10/M13/M17 and spindle nut size.
- Most common Allen bolt tools to fit casings.
- Multi-bit screwdriver or similar, with magnetic head.
- Plug spanner and spare plug(s).
- Pliers or, preferably, a quality multi-tool.
- Adjustable wrench.
- Tyre-repair kit and levers or puncture-repair spray.

The quest for tools can end up taking over a shed and keeping it all tidy becomes a full-time job. Do not worry if tools and parts end up scattered around while work is in flow; just set aside some time to re-establish (temporary) order every now and then.

Always have a couple of split chain links spare, with one in your travelling toolkit. Make sure they are good quality, as they could – quite literally – be the weakest link in the chain.

Always fit the round end of the clip facing the direction of travel. The clip fits over one pin and is pushed sideways into the slot of the other by pliers or a flat-blade screwdriver.

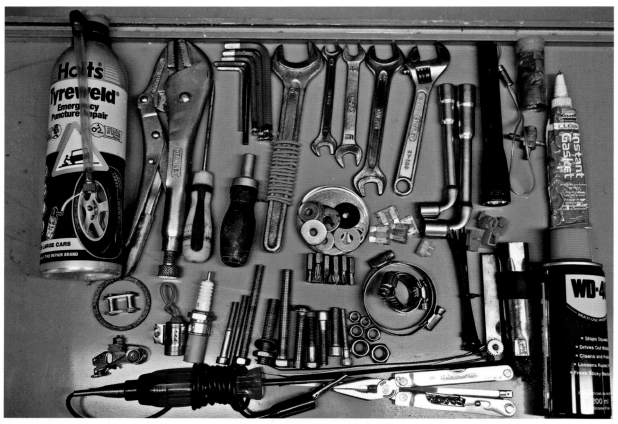

Preparation for a journey on a shed-built bike should include a decent toolkit. It may seem a lot to carry, but it should fit easily into a small bag or roll.

- Fuses and roll of electrical wire.
- Handful of cable ties.
- Plumber's mate epoxy putty, or similar.
- Small tube of gasket goo/silicone.
- Length of gaffer tape rolled around something or stuck in layers on the tool-roll.

- Strip of emery cloth 120/240 grit and feeler gauges.
- Couple of pairs of disposable gloves, and a tube of hand cleaner.
- Small can of WD40.

This is the kit I take if I am travelling any distance or length of time from home.

Depending on how self-sufficient I want to feel, I would also throw in some nuts and bolts, jubilee clips and a torch… and some emergency (calming) cigarette tobacco and a lighter for that period of time when I am waiting for the last, most important, tool to turn up: the emergency breakdown company.

Sunshine and the open road beckon; time to start work…

PROJECT: CAFÉ RACER

A true child of the baby boom, the café racer was all about speed and rebellion, taking the lumpy post-war bikes and shaping them into a statement of teenage rebellion. Never before had there been such wealth and freedom offered to the youth; the nascent teenager scene full of grit and revolt was to become a nationwide epidemic that was infected with a love of speed and freedom. Not for these working-class heroes the angst of being angry young men spouting prose or avant garde art at university and nice parties; no, they got down and dirty in sheds at the bottom of gardens arrayed behind the terraced streets of industrial Britain to create dreams in steel and leather. Here were born the daredevil riders ready to take advantage of the country's newly surfaced roads ringing towns and cities; an unregulated network of race-track to do the ton on, escaping the grind of the workplace.

Mass-manufactured parts weren't available in those days, it was all in the hands of self taught mechanics and builders, The base machines, raw and

The classic café racer, a BSA 650 twin sitting in a Norton frame. Nortons were considered the best-handling of the post-war British bikes and their frames were often used by builders. Build-wise, it ticks every box on the café racer list: twin leading shoe front brake, cut-down front mudguard, clip-ons, sculpted tank, shapely seat hump, sexy sweep to the exhaust and lovely rearsets, all set in classic lines. The benchmark for a café racer should always be this marriage of solid engineering and deceptively simple elegance.

The modern interpretation of café racers has produced 'street-fighters': powerful, modern motors with tweaked running gear, the evolutionary process easy to see. For some though, the handling and speed factors occasionally take a back seat to the wow factor; this Harley-engined beast, for example. A stunning frame design and use of metal makes this look the business. Twin leading shoe brakes were the height of stopping power in their day, then discs came along to show them how it should be done, the choice of anyone wanting to remove speed from a fast bike; whereas this lovely looking set-up may not be up to the job. The disparity in width of the tyres may make quick cornering a process to remember; they will work fine but are not a performance mod.

ripe for exploitation, were pulled apart, ready to lay out thin seats, slender tanks and cut down ancillaries over bastardized hybrids of pokey engines and track-proven frames; spartan imitations of the racing bikes hammering around the official courses on public roads throughout the land. Boys with dirt under their nails cut down and modded the standard road trimmings using the engineering skills everyone learned at school, hammering and welding veritable silk purses from sows' ears.

The contrast with the biking scene across the Atlantic couldn't have been more marked; healthy well-fed Yanks sat high and back on heavyweight cruisers built to be comfortable over great distances across the American continent, knees in the breeze and beer in the belly, while skinny, pale Brits hunkered down over lightweight missiles ducking and diving through the narrow streets and lanes of a small wet island, acne scarred from poor diets and spending nights clustered in cafes around a cup of tea and packet of Woodbines.

On the Right Lines

Getting the lines of a café racer is quite an important step. It needs to be speedy-looking and compact, with the frame and engine level, or slightly canted forward. This means that the forks should not be over-long; they can be dropped in the yokes to shunt the weight of the rider over the engine, keeping the mass central. The bottom edge line of the tank and seat should be straight, running from front to rear, and once again horizontal, or lower at the front. Fuel

taps are usually at the rear of tanks so, unless the outlet can be moved, it will need to be at the lowest point. The seat base should come up to the tank, taking the bottom of the tank line to the hump over the back wheel, with the unit ending just past the axle line. If it is too short, it will look and be cramped; if it is too far back, that will upset the stance.

Top Lines

Tanks should be slim and long, preferably with cut-outs for the knees, so the rider can get well tucked in, and the rear edge dropping down to the seat. This should have a thin padding rising up the hump at the rear with very little shaping – basically, it is a slab of covered foam with the merest nod to comfort. To mount the seat securely it may be necessary to chop the rear rails about, cleaning and extending them, or incorporate a new loop; the seat and tank should be acquired as early as possible in the process and set up as desired. During the mock-up build, anything that gets in the way of mounting the seat and the tank can be cut off – but only up to a point. Major structural tubes should not be attacked unless a radical frame alteration is on the cards

Wheels

Modern sports bikes have a large wheel at the back, to lay down power and provide plenty of rubber on the road, and a smaller and narrower one at the front, to reduce mass and make for tight, accurate tracking. This contrasts with the classic look of skinny, 18- or 19-inch wheels, approximately the same size front and rear, with only slightly wider boots on the rear. Deciding on the wheels, trying to get a matching pair – whether cast or spoked – will help set the tone of the bike, giving it an elegant classic feel or modern performance looks.

Ergonomics

If the original or modified wheels, suspension and fork set-up are to be kept, they can be used to build the rolling mock-up with tank and seat in place; this will also help in finding alternative components, as it will allow sizes and travel to be worked out. Now the ergonomics can be figured out – a

Modern Norton with an interesting style of rearset. The curved actuating rod and the vectors involved look to be at the very edge of usefulness; good lever design must always ensure they work well.

A Buell motor in a modded Harley frame, with old-school tank and seat, gives a good classic look to Chris's bike. The steering damper is a good choice to use with narrow twitchy bars on largish diameter wheels. Homemade headers join into a nice reverse-cone mega that sends out a sweet rumble through the lanes of France.

mixing and matching

Obviously, it is possible to mix and match components – the successful marrying of seemingly disparate details is often the defining character of a custom bike; no two customs will ever be the same; each one will be a reflection of its creator. And that is truly the underlying satisfaction and joy of building a bike.

somewhat subjective exercise in engineering and layout design. Make sure the bike will not fall over, get some experienced help, or at least a spare pair of hands, if possible, and get on.

Riding Position

Lean forward and put your hands where they are comfortable at the yokes. Use a pair of clip-ons or clubmans for that authentic look, or a flat pair of drag bars on the top yoke. Make sure there is not too much strain on the wrists as that is where the weight of the body will be carried. Consider the clearance for the clip-ons at full lock; make sure nothing comes into contact with the tank and that you can turn the bike with both hands able to use the controls.

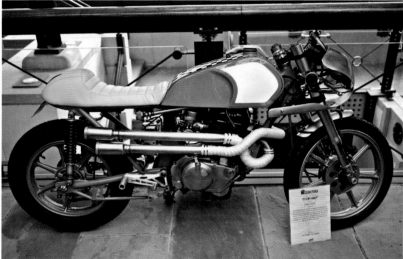

TOP AND MIDDLE: Two bikes, both sporting what could be termed the custom café-racer style: the one above is purposeful and this function gives it form, creating a machine that looks cool and useful. That below is a bizarre mash-up of parts. At the front, the fairing is set too low; hard braking will probably push the pilot's chest on to the protruding bolt atop the gas tank, and having an oil breather next to the white seat is asking for trouble. Exhaust wrap can actually damage pipes; if it is an attempt to make the bike look like an old-school racer, it should at least be put on correctly…

BOTTOM LEFT: The 'Kettle', an early Japanese water-cooled 750 two-stroke triple, is an iconic machine and makes a superb café racer. Brakes and rolling gear are all top stuff; with USD forks and monoshock conversion, this is a serious attempt at a fast bike that handles well. The acres of shiny metal give it an impressive presence, as does the incredible noise from the expansion pipes.

Foot controls should be easy to work and not placed too far forward. Stock controls and their position might work for a while but for any serious riding the feet need to be further back, to give the correct body lean. If the passenger pegs are still on, try these as a reference for mounting rearsets, or get a friend to hold a bar in a place where everything sits right and the feet can rotate to operate the brake and gears. Make sure the knees will not be banging on parts of the engine or carbs, and that the run of the exhaust will not interfere with the movement of the brake and gear levers.

Footwork

The footpeg and controls' mount, perhaps on a back plate that attaches to existing location holes, or tack-on brackets where needed, should be strong enough to take the rider's weight without flexing, yet not look too bulky. As an alternative to making up a bespoke set, have a look around at the aftermarket rearsets available, or use second-hand bits from another bike.

The gear lever will need to be linked to the new lever by a stiff bar, with a connection that allows movement; this could be either using clevis or ball joint on the ends of the rod. The leverage lengths should be similar to ensure correct operation; be prepared to make a couple of attempts to get this right.

tidying up the basics

Whether the bike you have bought is a new one or a standard second-hand machine, it's possibly been purchased viewed through rose-tinted goggles in terms of how cool you think you will look as you cruise down the street on it. It is fair to say that, when a bike is bought, it is more about looks than anything else. Sadly, as in many love affairs, once the first glow has dimmed, the effort of ignoring all the shortcomings of your chosen one can lead to depression, remorse and possibly rejection.

Never fear! While it may be impossible to turn the person on the other side of the breakfast table into a dreamboat, it is possible to improve the most important thing in your life: let's get into customizing.

Bikes are put together in the factory using the cheapest components that will do the job – a truism for the most expensive down to the cheapest – and they are also designed to be easy to put together. Things are not always as tidy as they might be if someone with flair had designed them. Standard advertising pics tend to have the bike in shadow to make it look cool, and will often airbrush or Photoshop out the untidy bits. Closer inspection may reveal many things that just do not measure up.

TOP RIGHT: Fresh-looking engine after vapour blast clean. A running engine that was very grubby, rather than strip it down it was decided to clean as a unit; a risky exercise, but it can be done. The issue here is to prevent any abrasive material getting into the motor, so it had to be completely sealed. Any blast abrasive getting onto bearing surfaces or moving parts will destroy them, so care is needed.

RIGHT: A customized bike with some serious money spent on flash bits, but a basic improvement has been missed: all the fasteners are still stock cadmium-plated cheap versions from the factory that will, in a couple of seasons, become grotty and corroded. Details such as this distinguish builders who want to improve their bike from those who are more concerned with image.

These lovely Ceriani forks are highly covetable for anyone wanting to give kudos to a flat-tracker.

An engine rebuild at Redmax – a box full of stainless bolts stands ready to replace the standard ones. It does not add significantly to the cost, but it is a sign of a consistency in the approach to the work.

CHANGING THE BIG THINGS

A bike is a pretty generic item: a frame, an engine and wheels at either end. With such a simple format, changing a couple of larger components can wholly alter the genre, but not the quality. It is important to consider that, apart from the tank, seat and handlebars, everything else is designed to make that particular bike go, handle and stop safely, while achieving a decent level of performance and reliability from the powerplant.

Aftermarket parts are probably the easiest way to go. They tend to be designed to replace standard bits with minimal hassle, such as mounting points and size. But they are generic and usually represent someone else's idea of what looks good on a bike. They do tend to come with their own instructions, but it may be useful to give them a once-over and exchange fasteners for stainless, remove any casting marks and just tidy them up generally.

NUTS AND BOLTS

Fasteners are the most obvious starting point when tidying up your purchase. Standard nuts and bolts are generally steel, and on older bikes they will be all rusty and grimy. Shiny new zinc or chrome ones will go the same way, so it is best to replace them with stainless steel. This will ensure they stay as shiny as you want, and will help you in future work on the bike as they should not corrode and lock up.

Aside from old British and American, all bikes use metric threads, so, rather than buying an expensive set for your particular bike, find a local fastener supplier where shopping is a pleasant recreation for gearheads. There, you can browse the shelves of shiny bits and bobs, often finding nice surprises – yes, the internet can supply many things, but it is not the same as actually fondling metal. Either measure or take in the originals and get one-for-one replacements. Socket- or Allen-headed bolts and locking nuts with the appropriate washers represent a cost-effective route to follow. Once you have started, you will probably optimistically end up with every fastener on the bike changed for top quality. There are two grades of stainless: A2 (304) is the cheaper one, supplied in a greater range and perfectly usable for bikes; A4 (316) is the top grade, for food and marine applications, which is much pricier but impervious to corrosion.

Titanium bolts are rust-free, light and super strong. Use where weight is at a premium, and money is not.

how to remove a stud

Stud requiring removal.

Thread two nuts on to the stud.

Tighten against each other, then undo with a spanner on the lower nut.

Fasteners can also be had in aluminium, brass and bronze, although the range is limited and not as strong as steel. They can, however, add nice detailing to a project in non-stressed applications.

It is cost-effective when buying fasteners to get them in multiples of ten (unless you need a really specific size that cannot be used anywhere else) – the unit price comes down substantially, and a good range of spare fasteners is always useful. Certain components on a bike will have a different thread pitch (the distance between the thread); for example, spindles, brake mounts and shocks are finer, to provide greater locking security. Such items can be harder to find locally, so go online and search for them, buying through a custom supplier or bike shop will add substantially

ABOVE: A thread gauge used for measuring the pitch of threads, here with three metric threads of different pitches.

BELOW: A morning spent browsing the shelves of a local supplier could provide all the nuts and bolts needed for a once-in-a-bike-lifetime transformation, making future disassembly hassle-free.

43

Wire locking of fasteners is a competition trick that is handy for bikes on the road, especially those that vibrate a lot. The specially drilled nuts are pricey, but will only ever be bought once and provide a lovely detail.

to the price, and they'll be getting theirs from the same large suppliers available to you online. Ask for a catalogue from the online supplier, to make life easier if you find yourself searching often. An 800-page catalogue that gives all dimensions, materials and, usefully, the correct names for a multitude of fasteners will sit nicely on a shelf in the smallest room for leisurely browsing.

Engine-cover or case bolts can be swapped over without removing the cover. This will avoid bother if the cover or case has components locked in or is full of oil. First, sketch a diagram of the cover, to record the location and number of the bolts in order, say, clockwise from the top. Take out the first one, measure the shank and thread length (from under the head to the end in millimetres), check the size – M4/M5/M6 – write it down on the diagram and replace it, pinched tight; repeat the requisite number of times, then go shopping.

When it comes to doing the replacements, remove the old bolt, clean out any gunge from the recess with a wad of hand towel or a squirt of WD, let it soak and blow out with an airline – be careful not to get anything in your eyes. Apply a drop of Loctite on the thread of the new bolt and take it in to pinch pressure (tight without applying leverage). Do this for the whole cover and then torque all the bolts up tight. For the heads and some other parts, there may be a specific sequence to undoing and tightening, so check in the manual first.

If a bolt or piece of studding is too long, cut it to size, but be aware that the thread can become mangled during cutting and will not thread in properly. It is all too easy to cross-thread when putting into alloy, so always try the newly cut thread with a nut to check.

To cut on a lathe, use a parting tool to completely cut it off, or make a groove deeper than the thread and cut with a fine-tooth hacksaw, then turn an angled end on it to clean up the thread.

If using a vice, thread a nut on past the cut, secure in the vice and cut off with a hacksaw or fine cutting disc; taking the nut off will pull the distorted end back into life. The end can be burnished on a fine grinding wheel by holding it at about 60 degrees and rotating as it grinds.

BRAKING SYSTEM
Brake Lines

Hydraulic brake lines, as originally fitted, tend to be black rubber hose with steel fittings terminating in metal pipes that feed into the calipers. They are cheap and prone to grubbiness and corrosion, with threaded parts often corroding up together, making removal impossible without mangling the nut. Replacing

Clean bolt ends: (right) as bought; (centre) the finish from a hacksaw or disc, sharp and difficult to thread on; (left) a cut bolt finished off by a bench grinder and cleaned up using the thread file.

ABOVE: Calipers are stuck out in the elements and may be vulnerable. On the component on the right, line connections, pins (examples at the front) and fasteners are all corroded, making any servicing and smooth functioning an uncertainty. They need to be replaced with stainless. New pins can be purchased online, whereas these have been turned from socket bolts, costing a fraction of the price.

RIGHT: Made-to-order custom bike with built-in problems: the kinked oil line and connector held in with PTFE tape do not bode well, while the spaghetti of wiring under the tank is exposed to the elements and may become a problem in the future. As usual, bling is not necessarily better.

them with stainless braided line and decent ends, either with a shiny metal finish or cased in a black or coloured outer, is simple to do and looks good. It will also significantly improve the working life of the braking system.

To determine the length needed, use a piece of three-core electric cable, thread it from the master cylinder, through the various places where the brake line must run, attaching it where necessary (bars, yokes, and so on) with cable ties or masking tape to get the true length, right down to the caliper.

After mounting the engine in a frame for mocking up, the next thing is to sort out where the battery is going. Make a cardboard or wooden box larger than the battery, to try out mounting places. Haphazard or unsightly positioning often gives away the fact that someone has built a bike and forgotten this until too late.

For twin discs, go to where the splitter junction is mounted, then take two lines down to the calipers. Measure the length of line needed from the cable mock-up, ensuring that the forks are fully extended and that the handlebars can be turned in both directions without pulling or snagging the cable.

With this information and the make of bike and caliper, send off to a reputable supplier who can make up a line with the correct fittings. Always use stainless steel, as chrome looks cheap and plated steel goes horrid. Have a banjo junction at the bars and a straight into the caliper/splitter box, as two straights will require dismounting either the cylinder or caliper to thread in both ends, which is a pain. It is possible to make up lines at home; it is a bit fiddly, but it can help if you are doing something interesting such as threading the line through a hole in the yokes. Be sure to order stainless bleed nipples at the same time.

Fitting Brake Lines

Encase the caliper in baking foil and masking tape, and cover the rest of the bike directly below the caliper with rag so that no brake fluid gets on the disc, fork leg, rim and tyre. Cover the bars and anything below the cylinder with rag as well. Use a good length of clear windscreen-washer tube, with one end on the bleed nipple and the other into a waste container. Undo the nipple and operate the brake to pump all the fluid out of the system. Pinch the tube next to the nipple, remove it and let the fluid drain away. Wearing disposable gloves and using a handy mop-up rag, undo the fittings at both ends, remove the bleed nipple and ditch the lot.

Attach the new fittings to the caliper and cylinder, using new copper washers that squish down to seal the join. If you only have used copper washers, they can be re-annealed by heating to

An OEM brake line stretched too tight should be replaced with a stainless braided line and stainless connections.

RIGHT: Being mild steel, the connections are prone to corrosion and seizing up, making removal difficult.

BELOW LEFT: Cutting the line to length using heat-shrink wrapping to prevent fraying; tape will do as well. A thin cutting disc is best. Snips may crimp and fray and, while careful cutting with a hacksaw is possible, the teeth can snag the braid.

ABOVE: Banjo connectors: one is the fixed type, which allows the line to be removed from it, the other has the tube fixed to the line by the lock nut. The brass olive is held inside the join.

LEFT: Remove the heat-shrink and slide the lock nut over the line with the thread at the cut end. Gently pry the braid away from the cut end and push the olive over the plastic inner until it is snug.

Slide the lock nut up over the olive, insert the connection tube into the plastic inner and screw up by hand. Keep pressure on the connection so that the lock nut does not dislodge the olive. This is another connection type that screws into the cylinder or caliper.

ABOVE: *When all is set up, tighten using a spanner. Some will need the connection part to be held by a spanner. When tightening a banjo, as here, do not clamp it in a vice, as any marks may cause a leak.*
RIGHT: *Install the connector using new copper washers, holding it in position while tightening, to prevent it rotating and pulling the line. The bleed nipple has been replaced with a stainless one and comes with a rubber cap to keep dirt out.*

Twin leading shoes double the effectiveness of the lowly drum brake. Here, Jen has cleaned and rebuilt the classic wheel with stainless spokes, adapting it to fit USD forks. Note all the fasteners are stainless.

red on a gas flame then quenching in cold water. Once you have wiped off the black residue, they will be soft and usable again.

Bleeding

Take the new nipple back one turn or so, and attach the clear pipe. Fix the pipe so that it is straight up to the height of the cylinder and tape a bit of soak-up rag just down from the open end. Filling the cylinder as it empties, calmly pump the brake until fluid appears in the pipe.

Holding the lever in, nip up the nipple, release the lever and pump a couple of times. The caliper should be well on its way to full and then all that is needed is to bleed the air out. If you open the nipple and squeeze the lever, air should push up the pipe in the fluid; with the lever held in, nip up and let the bubbles float upwards. Repeat calmly until no more air exits the caliper and pulling in the lever gets harder, indicating the caliper is in working order.

This is one method for bleeding. There are others that use one-way valves or airlock bottles – find the one that works for you.

Neatly attach the cable to its chosen route with small cable ties or clips, and stand back and admire your handiwork.

MAINTENANCE AND MODIFICATION

Replacing the fasteners and improving the braking system are detailing tasks that can be done without even mentioning the word 'custom'. However, it is important to go this way and have the basics covered. Even after such modest tweaking, any further work and maintenance on the machine will be easier, and the simple spannering involved builds tool skills and allows you to get a closer look at the bike. It may be that, apart from the tidying up, you have yet to decide what to do with it. It may turn out to be an evolutionary project, with any

Glorious in its simplicity, this rigid Panhead is the result of just the right amount of TLC and a few modifications, creating a seriously cool ride.

Splodge the dog guarding Pete's Gas'd Rat, a world-class show bike (third in the 2013 AMD World Championship). No one starts out as a professional custom bike builder – it is a title that must be earned – but everyone begins with shed builds, a love of detail and a desire to learn skills and acquire a deep knowledge of the bikes.

changes occurring over time, but in the meantime it needs to be used. The next stages involve getting the best from the bike and becoming familiar with it, and identifying what it might benefit from. Sometimes, it is better to hold fire on the full customization and just get it into peak condition.

Maybe your bike is an old(ish) air-cooled model that was bought as a runner. Before the customizing starts, it is a worthwhile exercise to get the best in terms of performance from it. This does not mean loading the bike up with high-performance parts; rather, it means following a to-do list that will get it working at optimum levels. The following advice should also be followed during the overall custom project; neglecting it may not lower the bike's aesthetic appeal but it might lead to a job half done, and possibly a machine that is a danger to ride. Quintessentially, this is maintenance that should be carried out on a regular basis. The reality is that it is all too easy simply to ride the bike, then stick it in the shed reeking of the road, in the hope that magic elves will have sorted everything out by the time the sun comes out again.

Out of the box and out of line – even top-of-the-range custom parts can be wrong. This ceramic exhaust system is never going to fit the bike for which it was sold. Some suppliers will not offer a refund if the component has been fixed, even if it has been found wanting.

Pattern Parts

There are plenty of cheap replacement and 'performance' parts available for bikes. Many come from dubious sources, making components that look like the original, from poorer-quality materials. The watch word here is *caveat emptor*, so always ask around or check on forums. That said, bearings, seals and electrical components are fairly universal items and, if you take the original to a large established supplier of these, or get the sizes and contact them, it should be possible to save a bit over the bike manufacturer's price. OEM do not usually make these in-house; the bike is designed to accept items that can be acquired off the shelf rather than only unique (and costly) ones. The part number will be stamped somewhere (usually very small) and can be used to carry out an online search – it will probably be out there somewhere.

Tyres

There is a wide choice of tyres, but you should never compromise safety in favour of looks.

Whatever size wheels are being used, they need to be shod with the best rubber you can afford, appropriate to the needs of the bike. It may look really funky to have a pair of huge balloon tyres all retro with old-style tread patterns and squared-off profiles, but it is not an exaggeration to say that they will literally let you down. Tyres are the only things stopping you sliding uncontrollably when you brake, corner or pull away, so, unless you have a death wish, go modern. There are loads of cool-looking and well-proven tread patterns out there.

Do not mix up types. For somebody who actually likes to ride a bike and get some excitement out of it, the sight of a knobbly on the front and a sidecar tyre on the back of a pokey hog, or similar mash-up, is a sure sign of an accident waiting to happen. If you think their bike looks cool, follow them on a rainy day; when they spill on a slimy manhole cover as the rubber fails at different levels, you can offer them a good price for the wreckage and you could get a bargain. Joking aside, while having a custom bike is all about making a statement that you are not happy to ride something that is normal, or often sensible, you should never compromise on tyres.

Unless it is for a show bike or one that will only ever be ridden on good, dry surfaces, the old-style and potentially dangerous tyres should be left at the garage. There are websites of 'top café racer and custom builders' who sell bikes with daft tyres to first-time riders; this is greed, hype and idiocy all rolled into one. Rather than blaming themselves, learner riders should understand the sad fact that there are dealers around who are prepared to sell something so unsuitable to them.

Good tyres, at the correct pressure, will improve handling and confidence, as well as prolonging life (yours). Buy a digital tyre gauge and use it once a week.

Brakes

Modern brakes are excellent and old ones tend to be rubbish by comparison, so make sure you are using the best for your bike. Confidence that you can pull up short, or apply the anchors while heeled over without locking up – silly tyres will be no help here – adds to the riding experience as the ride becomes smoother and quicker.

Even if the bike is old, decent-quality brake pads based on modern technology will make quite a difference. The popular classics, such as the 500/650 Yams, air-cooled Beemers or Sportsters, *et al.* have a large following, which has

resulted in many smart engineers producing good-quality upgrades.

Cables

Most people do not change cables, or even notice them, until they stop functioning. This means that, as they get worse, the rider is unaware of the gradual decline in performance, simply adjusting their style to suit. A gummed-up brake or throttle cable restricts the action needed to go and stop, but it will still work; however, the difference between the movement of a new cable

and that of one that is twenty-plus years old will be startling. Swap all cables for new, and it will feel like the bike has had a tune-up. Maintain them properly with a cable oiler and use very thin oil, as thick oils will trap dirt and clog up. Competition riders will clean through and oil cables after every meet. There is no need to be quite that keen, but it is worth trying to do it on a regular basis.

The OEM rubber hydraulic lines will begin to impart sponginess to braking and corroded parts will make care and repair difficult, so it is definitely worth changing up.

Upgrading brakes can often require engineering skills – here, a homemade bracket has been used to mount a decent caliper on to the lugs for the original. Accuracy and strength are paramount when altering such an important component, so measure three times, cut once and do it again if it is not perfect.

spindle removal

In the process of changing wheels, tyres or brakes, the spindle has to come out. Due to its location and tight fit, it can become corroded or just seized in place. If it looks like it is stuck, loosen off the nuts and clamps and get the thin pipe on your WD40 to spray into the interior at least a couple of hours before work.

Place a piece of hardwood or thickish alloy on the end and give it a clout with a big hammer. Do not hit it with metal on to the thread, as this will damage it. If it is threaded on both ends, put spacers below the nut and tighten to draw it through; you might need to grip the other end to stop it turning. Once it is moving and has disappeared into the wheel, use a bolt or bar smaller than the hole and drive it through. If the spindle is not too corroded, put it in the lathe and clean it with wire wool, but do not score it or remove metal.

A quick-action throttle is a simple improvement for a staid bike, giving a sharper response to each twist of the wrist and quite useful around town.

The ingredients of the helicoil box; an essential in the shed.

The guts from a pair of shocks off the same bike: one side still had a trace of oil in and looked reasonable; the other was in terrible condition, as the oil disappeared years ago, to be replaced by moisture. With some diligent cleaning, new seals and oil, coupled with a paint job or polish to the outers, they should be good for another ten years.

New Threads

Sometimes, the thread inside a hole will become chewed up (cross-threaded). If this happens, do not try to force the bolt – it may feel as though it has gripped, but will fail. The first repair attempt should be to chase the thread using the specific size tap or, preferably, a dedicated chaser. A quick-fix chaser can be made by grinding two grooves along a bolt to prevent clogging – it is not ideal, but it may work OK. Using taps, go in carefully with the tapered tap first, to get a good cutting position, and then use the middle tap. The problem here is that metal will be removed and the grip will be weakened.

The best solution is to use a helicoil, which is a coiled wire that forms a thread. Helicoil kits come with (top to bottom in the photo) a drill that goes in first removing the old thread and enlarging the hole; a tap to form a thread; and a tool that winds the helicoil into the threaded hole. The tang at the bottom is knocked off with the punch. The result is a sound and strong repair.

Suspension

Basically, the springy bits at the front and rear have a very big impact on how a bike handles, keeping the rider comfortable and ensuring that the wheels stay on the ground. At the front, drain the fork oil and top up with new. Check on a forum to see if different grades will suit a specific riding style and help damping. Progressive springs reduce the tendency of sharp diving under braking and rough surfaces, which alters the bike geometry. Check the stanchions for oil deposits above the sliders, as this will indicate that the seals are letting out oil that should be inside. If this is the case, change them. If there is pitting on the stanchion below the travel of the sliders, the seals will wear out more quickly.

Rear shocks start to become slack after time, especially after thirty years, which is about the average age of the classic bikes used for most customs; the problem is that this happens inside, while outside they continue to look fine. Do not buy shocks just because they look nice. They are all designed for specific bikes and weights, so sexy 125 motocross shocks on a 650 that weighs

Old-school bearings – so awkward, so wrong, so replace with modern.

Centres of wheel bearings have a spacer tube between them. This is essential to prevent distortion when tightening up the spindle, so do not forget it!

twice as much will be a disaster. Do some research and, if you buy the best quality you can, the difference will be noticeable.

Most shocks are rebuildable; the job will cost about the same as acquiring a generic cheap-to-average pair new. Rebuilding can, with patience and the right tools, be done at home. The bits that go are replaceable seals, while springs that have lost spring, as well as being corroded, can be purchased separately.

Bearings

Without bearings, a motorbike would not exist. They are essential to everything that goes round, but they are often neglected to the point of being rendered dangerous. When doing any work on the bike, if you happen across a bearing, take the opportunity to check it. Rotate the inner race, which should be held surely in place with no side movement. It should run smooth and silent; if it wobbles, clicks, grinds or makes a noise, replace it. To be properly conscientious, if you are not sure that it is a recent bearing, or if the bike is old, replace it as a matter of course.

Older bikes used ball-bearings in the headstock races, where protection from the elements was minimal. Road grit and water would mix with the grease to produce a nice grinding paste. The usual answer to this was to tighten down the spindle bolt to reduce slop or use a steering damper; eventually they would be too far gone,

making the front end unstable and handling dodgy. Nowadays, there are replacement bearings for just about every bike made that has a removable race (removable because this had to be tougher metal than the frame). Modern bearings are taper rolling, giving more stable handling, and installation is so much easier compared to praying that two sets of loose ball bearings, held in place with a dollop of grease, stay there while the yokes are slid through and fastened.

The same goes for swing arms, which are usually bushes or needle-roller bearings. Clean them thoroughly, check them and replace the bearing surfaces.

Air Filters

To work properly, a bike needs precise amounts of fuel and air. The system is easily compromised and should be checked if the bike feels sluggish, has flat spots or runs out of steam. Take down the carb and check the condition; grime builds up and clogs jets, needles wear out and seals go. The fuel tap should also be pulled as the filter is easily covered in debris from corrosion in an old tank. Get everything vapour-blasted (remembering to blow all the detritus out afterwards, using an airline), or sonic-cleaned, renew the internals and seals. Carb refurb kits,

This is getting serious: a carb in a supercharger system, giving serious oomph to a bike.

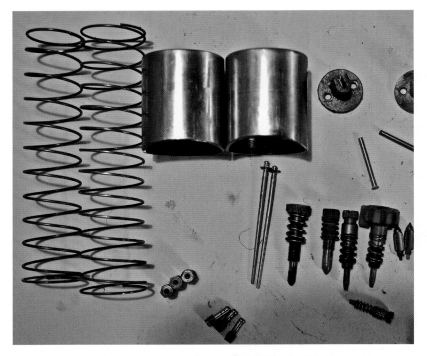

LEFT: A bargain pair of carbs proved to be less of a deal than they seemed at first. Although the bodies were identical, once stripped down they were found not to be the same, with different-length springs, slide cut-outs, jets and needles. It meant having to buy all new parts.

BELOW LEFT: Exhaust end caps turned on the shed lathe hold in the perforated tube that (slightly) reduces the volume. The mounting plate for the brake caliper was drawn from a cardboard template and cut by waterjet in stainless steel.

available from the manufacturers, contain all the bits needed.

Air filters fitted by manufacturers need to be cleaned or replaced when servicing. If they are dirty or clogged they will reduce airflow and inhibit performance. If the original filter system is being binned, make sure that the new one will be freer-breathing. It may be necessary to consider altering the jetting in the carbs, as more air can make the bike run leaner and hotter.

Exhausts

Standard exhausts are made to comply with regulations regarding noise and noxious vapour emissions, which translates to quiet and stifling; nowadays, modern Harleys and Triumphs sound as raunchy as a Honda Dream. If the bike is breathing in more, then a zortier exhaust will help it breathe out better and increase power. Be aware of the pitfalls of simply taking out the baffles or sticking on some drag-pipes; if the back pressure is lost, then power in certain areas will go as well. In addition, the bike will run leaner, so the fuel/air mix needs to be richer, necessitating more carb work.

The added bonus of a deeper growl and beat is good, but some consider it anti-social and occasionally it may even be illegal. If you cause excessive noise, you may have to learn how to charm your way through a vehicle test, or out of a ticket from the Old Bill.

SECOND-HAND SHOPPING

The Autojumble

Today, finding those elusive parts for the dream bike is just a mouse-click away, with a multitude of online shops and auction sites offering just about any

Modestly tweaked, bling-free, and ready for some of the twistier bits of the Pyrenees, Will's Triumph is a good example of customization for fun on the road.

A good autojumble or swap meet is the best place to find unusual or fitting items for the imaginative custom builder on a budget.

part second-hand or new. The problem is that you may not always know what you want, and it is hard to tell from a flat photo on a screen exactly what an item is like physically. The alternative and most sociable way is to go to an autojumble, or swap meet, to root out and actually hold a part, or lay hands on a tank, frame or complete bike.

Autojumbles are held across the country, often as a part of a motorcycle event, where shed builders can sell their unwanted items to other shed builders. Such events offer more than just shopping, though. They are a great place to ask for advice, meet like-minded souls and discover resources that can help complete a build. Wandering around one of these meets can be overwhelming to the uninitiated, but, once you find your feet, they can be a treasure trove.

While you may not know exactly what make or model component you need, you will know that you need it, but turning up without basic information could end up with you buying the wrong size or missing a bargain. Arm yourself before you go with dimensions – for a tank, for example, that would mean the length, the width of the tunnel, the height at the front and the back – and do some research on the rough price that your desired item might go for. Do this for all items that do not have an easily identifiable origin. Ask vendors if they have the piece you need or if they know of someone who does. You will find there is quite a network once you get involved, with people often able to track down elusive parts – and usually at a better price than online. You also get the chance to talk with someone on the same wavelength as yourself, who might be able to offer alternatives, give advice, or warn you about any problems you might encounter with your proposed build.

Take a decent amount of cash, a sturdy bag and warm clothes – it is hard to concentrate when you are standing in a freezing wind. Many autojumbles also feature sellers of new parts, from spark plugs, levers, mudguards, electrical components and sundries such as cleaning kits, tools and oils. To make the most of this, compose a list of what the bike uses; prices might be slightly higher than they would be online, but there will be no postage to pay and it will all be at hand.

If a suitable pair of shocks exist, somewhere like this will be the place to look.

Breakers

In the old days, there used to be a breaker's or salvage yard in almost every town, but the conveniences of buying and selling online have put paid to most of them. If you do find one, it is worth cultivating a good relationship with the owners (who are quite likely to be shed builders themselves). Discussing your plans and showing some photos will be a good starting point. The added advantage of these places is that there should be none of the bargain-hunting haste of the autojumble.

Often, they will have stock that is not on display, and if you are lucky you might gain access to the hidden treasure trove. If you are looking for a tank, for example, ask to see a couple that may fit the bill. If you remain undecided, see if you can take them home to try up; a deposit will be payable, but if the owners are decent you will not have to pay for what you do not use. Another upside is that they may be interested in buying the unused parts from your original bike, or, even better, offer part- exchange terms.

slipping screws

Cross-head and slot screws are sometimes found on bikes. If the screwdriver does not grip well, put some grinding paste in the set to help. Really stuck screws can be removed using an impact driver. If you do not have one of these, place a solid screwdriver in place and give it a thwack with a hammer to break the seal.

PROJECT: MAKING A SIMPLE CLAMP

After cleaning a frame and working out the location of mounting tabs, you may find that something has been forgotten. In getting the frame finished, all the main components will have been allocated a dedicated mounting point, but some of the ancillary stuff, such as oil pipes and wiring, will have been left dangling off, looking like an afterthought. Simply cable-tying these to a tube or another bit may be the easiest solution, but it is not the neatest. Much better to use cute little clamps, which look professional and are fairly easy to make.

This example is for an inline fuel filter, an essential bit of kit, especially if you are using an old tank that may be full of grot, holding it neatly and securely in place. There are many aftermarket suppliers that manufacture these and similar items, but if it is not the right size, or is in hideous chrome, you will end up having to mod it anyway. It will also have to be found, ordered and waited for, which can be frustrating for the less patient builder.

From my piles of odd bits of metal, scrounged from scrap bins, I found an aluminium disc that had roughly the right outside dimensions, and set to.

Noting the diameters of the frame tube and the filter, I centre-punched far enough in to give meat around the edges. The piece can then be set up for drilling or, as here, on a four-jaw chuck for the lathe.

To mount and find the centre you need, put a drill bit in the tailstock and use it to pin the metal to the chuck,

Fuel filter – essential but untidy.

correctly located by the bit in the centre punch mark. Then pull in the individual jaws until the piece is locked in place. Drill the holes, allowing a couple of mill over if possible, and repeat the process for the other hole(s); note the spare holes – these are purely decorative to give a more interesting shape.

If a lathe is not available it is easy enough to do the work in a pillar drill instead. It actually required less setting up, as long as the piece is held securely, to prevent it spinning out of control as the bit bites.

Once the holes have been drilled, the excess metal is cut off. When starting

Lined up in the chuck with centre-pop at centre of rotation.

All holes drilled.

with a disc shape, there is already a nice curve on the ends; when cutting from a different shape, some more meat will have to come off. Clean up the edges by grinding, filing and sanding until the surface is ready; a belt sander gives a nice finish. The metal will get hot very quickly, so wear gloves and leave it to cool when it is too much to handle.

Drill using the correct size bit for tapping in a thread (here, M6) at right-angles to the line from the centres of the main holes; this will be the joint line and this hole is for the bolt to hold the two halves together.

To cut it in two, mount in a vice or clamp a straight bar just off from the centre line and saw with a hacksaw held flat against the vice or bar as a guide. When it has been cut, clean up the mating faces lightly to remove burrs, but no meat.

Tap one side of the clamp and drill out the other to take the shank of the bolt; if needed, and there is enough meat, counterbore to set the head in flush.

Now clean up and finish the flat faces of the metal, to remove all working marks and any dints from the vice.

This technique can be adapted to take cables, wiring and oil pipes.

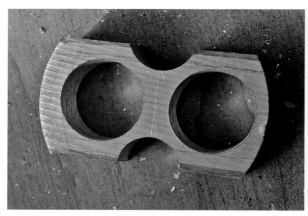

ABOVE: *Interesting shape, simply made.*
RIGHT: *Cutting in half; note hole for bolt.*

ABOVE: *Line the inner faces with some cloth tape to soften up the bite and fix in place.*
RIGHT: *The finished article.*

removing a broken stud

Removing a snapped stud depends on its size and how far out it projects. First, warm the metal it is in – this may allow mole grips or, preferably, a stud extractor to turn it out, as long as there is enough meat. If there is room, drop a nut over it and weld it to the stub, then turn out with spanner. When it has broken flush, use an easy-out extractor, by drilling in the centre; use the largest-diameter size, but do not go too big as the wall will be too thin and may wedge against the threads. As a last resort, try spark erosion, which involves mounting the metal in a machine and can be costly, or drilling out the whole stud and fitting a helicoil in.

PROJECT: TT500 SCRAMBLER

The scrambler style lends itself perfectly to the urban bike, with sharp acceleration, wide bars and a nimble setup making it ideal for blatting around streets and carving up traffic.

A good choice would be a torquey single, here the Yamaha 500 was the chosen bike; this approach would work with any of the alternatives, much work can be regarded as common to any similar build.

Because of its collectable value, a complete bike woud be an expensive option, especially as most of the standard kit would be binned. In this case, online shopping and trips to the breakers resulted in a good collection of the main components. This is a model that has been broken extensively over the years so most of the components can be found quite easily second-hand. A recent quick search online revealed the availability of more than thirty suitable frames, so there should be no problems there.

The standard dirt-bike frame of that era needs little work to trim it back to basics, and with the Yam having oil in

ABOVE: As far as minimalist bikes go, it is hard to beat the concept of an off-road competition machine. This Triumph twinshock scrambler is ready to have some dirty fun, with everything pared down to the minimum, while being tough enough to take some serious abuse.

RIGHT: The major parts for the project.

the frame, there was one less thing to find a place for when building the bike. By a stroke of luck and with some rooting around, a frame in fairly good condition was found buried in the ground of a small-town scrapyard. It had some surface rust to the bottom, but luckily it had the oil cap on, so there was no corrosion inside the oil reservoir.

Motor

A rebuilt engine with an oversize piston and decent cam for competition was a fortunate (but not rare) find on an internet auction site. Obviously, buying like this is a risk, but photos of the rebuild, the presence of new gaskets, and evidence of the builder's competence when viewing his workshop swung the deal.

The engine deserved to breathe better, so a carb was also bought online. It was the correct size but actually designed for a two-stroke, so it would have been unusable without a lot of work and had to be sidelined. A new flatslide Mikuni with accelerator pump was fitted; this came ready jetted for the engine, which made life a lot easier for tuning.

Suspension

Both front and rear suspension had to be sourced and, with an idea that big'n'beefy was the way to go, it was not difficult to find a nice aluminium mono-shock swing arm from a later motocrosser. The important point was that the spindle mount would fit in between the frame mounts – when searching for

XT frame with the rear loop cut off.

A shorter rear loop is fabricated and attached to the detabbed frame.

parts at a breaker's yard or autojumble, make a list of the dimensions needed for parts to mate up, and carry a tape measure and vernier caliper to get it exact.

Trueing up the swing arm involves putting a loose XT spindle, or appropriately sized rod if a spindle is not handy, through and using washers to space it exactly in the centre. Bronze bushes to fit were ordered from the internet, and end spacers and a central spacer were easily turned up from thick-wall aluminium tube to centre it. A grease nipple was tapped into this to allow the application of lube from the centre out.

The swing arm was longer than standard, so longer shocks could be used to kick the back end up; this would match up with the longer forks on the front and give the bike a lean, stretched stance with plenty of ground clearance.

It is also necessary to check the run of the chain so that the chain clears the swing arm and has a straight pull from sprocket to sprocket. This can be done by setting up the rear wheel or hub on a bar or spindle and sighting down with a straight edge.

Rather than mod the frame for monoshock, it would be easier to use

Big breather – a Mikuni Flatslide carb.

Riding in classic motocross on a similar bike will give a feel for the engine. Information from other riders led to a better oil-feed pipe being fitted, to lubricate the top end. Tips such as this can be easily found on forums.

Lining up a replacement swing arm; the monoshock mounts will be removed and twinshock attached.

ABOVE: Welding tabs in place with a TIG welder.

RIGHT: Locating mounts for shocks.

the existing shock mounts and weld mounts on the swing arm. To work out the shock angle, the frame was set on a box at approximately the right height, and the height of the wheel centres was worked out so that all would sit level. Shocks were fixed at the top and marked with a scribed line where they sat on the swing arm; ink marks should not be used as they can react with the weld and they also disappear when the metal gets hot.

Aluminium plate cut and drilled for the mount was bolted to the shock and set in place for welding. Really accurate scribes and locating marks need to be made to get it right. Use threaded bar with nuts to lock the tabs parallel and at the right distance apart when welding; this also helps to measure their trueness by coming off the swing-arm spindle equally.

Rather than relying on buying used shocks that would probably need a big clean-up, a new pair was bought online. They came nicely anodized, with painted springs, and looked rather impressive. Obviously, they were rated for the weight of the bike and rider.

Wheels

The plan was to have chunky 18-inch wheels front and rear, so a pair of moth-eaten rear wheels from the same period were bought for next to nothing. The spokes were rusty and loose and the bearings locked up, but the rims were true, with no damage and, being alloy, could be successfully polished out. One hub was in good condition, with flaking paint, and the other had a decent brake plate. A front wheel with a bent rim was acquired virtually free from the same yard. It is often sensible – or necessary – to cannibalize parts; in this case, two rough wheels could be had much more cheaply than one good one, which would probably need working on anyway.

Stainless spokes were ordered from one of the few shops that size up for the different rim/hub configurations. A photo was taken of the original spoke layout for reference, then the new spokes were put in place and, with the help of an experienced builder, laced up and trued. New bearings, oil seals and brake shoes completed the refurb, topped off with some big block road-legal enduro tyres.

Forks from a 1980s motocrosser were chosen from the many available, with big-diameter stanchions and long travel. (Being from a Yamaha YZ, they had the same lock for the brake plate and spindle diameter.) Condition was good, with no pitting to the legs and a usable spindle thread and clamp. After a strip down and a clean, new seals and fresh oil, they were as good as new. Because the front tyre was to be wider than standard, new yokes were designed and made.

Well worth a second look – the rim is true and the hub in good condition.

ABOVE: *Laying out the spoke pattern before adding the rim*
RIGHT: *A vapour-blasted and buffed alloy tank gives sculpted lines to the top of the bike.*

Yokes

As the bike was to have a wider front wheel and the fork legs were larger, standard yokes could not be used, so a pair had to be made. Self-designed, they were accurately cut from aluminium, then machined to fit. The cost was comparable to buying from a shop, but the result was something that was specifically tailored for the bike, and lovely besides. The new yokes were originally to be based on the layout of the ones from which the forks came, rather than the ones with the frame. This was because the forks had a leading spindle, while the XT forks had the spindle at the bottom of the forks. If the XT layout was used, the wheel would be kicked out compared to the standard; it was decided that this was a good thing as the bike was to be long, giving it a hint

Not quite a bespoke brat seat; as long as the base is good and the foam holds up, this is a good buy.

of hill-climber. Once the yokes were in the pipeline, the engine could be mounted in the frame and the dry build could be started in earnest.

Tank

A couple of tanks were being considered, both from early Yamaha motocrossers, and both alloy and sleekly shaped. The smaller was the same as the factory special HL540 and would give a pleasing nod to the racing heritage of these bikes; the colour and patina were gorgeous but, unfortunately, it only held about 30 miles' worth of juice. The other had had its tunnel replaced with one that sat over the frame and engine, was vapour-blasted and hand-polished.

Together, the tank and seat were what gave the bike its roots. The Yamaha single dirt bikes were all slender machines with fairly sculpted tanks and nicely rounded ribbed seats. A tatty DT175 seat was therefore offered up for size to the second tank. After new mounts were worked out, it was stripped down, the base painted and a pattern seat cover fitted.

Basics

All the fasteners were swapped out for stainless steel and inserted with a smear of copper grease, to prevent galvanetic reaction. New cables and fuel lines were put in place and the electric wires were replaced.

Coordinating second-hand levers were stripped down, polished, then assembled with new pivot bolts. The kill-button internals were cleaned of corrosion, then a new wire was soldered in and fitted to competition tapered motocross bars, with chunky Jackhammer-style rubber grips.

Footpegs from an early XS650 were welded on to the original stubs and new rubbers were fitted. Unfortunately, the kickstart travel meant that one of the pegs was continually bashed against, until it came loose, so it needed another mount to move it out of the way.

TOP RIGHT: *Good slender lines.*

BOTTOM RIGHT: *Snail-cam adjusters were mounted on the rear axle plates, by drilling and tapping a M6 hole and using a socket screw as the resting point.*

Tough and chunky grips with refurbished controls.

A bike can often be built using reclaimed and new parts for much less than it would cost to buy a standard running bike. Having a rough idea of the lines it should follow, with inspiration from classic models, meant that no time or effort were wasted creating a new concept. The finished machine is typical of shed-built mongrels put together with a limited budget, using common sense and basic workshop techniques.

controls

HANDLEBARS

Getting the right set of bars to work with your custom is not a hard task, as there are plenty of suppliers around. However, you will need to do some sorting out when changing them. Radical alterations can involve a significant amount of work, which can then throw up problems that prevent a quick fix. It is more or less impossible to knock up bars at home and, as there is probably a set out there to suit you, it is not really

metal matters

Bars come in three materials: steel, stainless steel and (aluminium) alloy. Choosing which metal to have is not always simple, especially if the chosen ones are limited in production.

Steel, usually chrome-plated or heavily painted, is the basic option. Second-hand ones are easy to come by, but any damage to the outer layer could mean corrosion, which will cost to repair. Easy to work and cheap, steel is used for the widest range of bars.

Stainless steel is a good choice. It is a bit heavy but it is not prone to corrosion and its mellower sheen is attractive compared to shiny chrome. Due to the cost and certain difficulties in working the material, the range of stainless-steel bars is a bit limited.

Alloy bars are light and easy to polish up when scratched. These are used in many performance applications, so the choice is quite good, but there is also a lot of cheap knock-off junk out there.

ABOVE RIGHT: Probably the easiest way to add some individuality to a bike is to change out the controls on the handlebars. Upgrading the standard components to performance kit will mean the bike goes and stops better, and adding a set of bespoke grips sets off the ensemble.

RIGHT: Shopping online for bars is easy, but, unless you know exactly what suits, it is better to get down and check out the range to see how they feel and look in the flesh.

Tapered motocross bars have a fat centre and with beefy clamps can fill out the space well. Here, all the wiring is running through the bars for a clean look. Tidying up the cables and wires allows the design to stand out without the distraction of clutter.

Clip-ons give a racing stance and, with rearsets, are de rigueur for a café racer. As they bring the hands down level with the tank, it is important that there is clearance when turning. It may be necessary to alter the steering stops to achieve this.

worth having them commissioned, unless you want to get really special.

Quick Style Checklist

- For café racers, it has to be clip-ons, straight bars or those weird clubman things.
- Trackers will have cowhorns – wide and not too high.
- Scramblers use cowhorns and MX bars of varying height and pullback.
- Chops are everything else, from ape-hangers to Z-bars.

It may be easy enough to indicate the different styles, but in fact there are no standard versions of these. There will be variations of rise, width and pullback for just about all manufacturers.

Dimensions

Road bars come in two sizes: $^7/_8$in (22 mm) for most bikes and 1in (25mm), used on Harleys and some modern big bikes. Using risers for attaching the bars, it's possible to have either; whereas clamps that are part of the yokes will dictate otherwise.

Dirt bikes also have a choice of tapered or fat bars that are large in diameter at the clamp and taper down to $^7/_8$in at the controls. This is my favourite look, followed by the 1-in, as they just fill out the space better.

Fitting

Give all the control housing screws a quick spray of penetrating oil (WD40) an hour before attempting any work; they are frequently cross-head screws, which corrode into the alloy and can be tricky to get out.

Use a screwdriver that fits exactly to remove the screws and note the length and size, to replace with stainless Allen bolts. Take off the housings and thread the screws back in to keep them safe. If the throttle and perches are such that they need to slide off, but the cables are not long enough, undo the clamps and move the bars around to allow this. Offer up the new bars to see if this operation needs to be reversed in order to get them on. This is often the case when putting wider or higher bars on.

Use new stainless bolts in the clamps, or wire-brush the threads clean on the

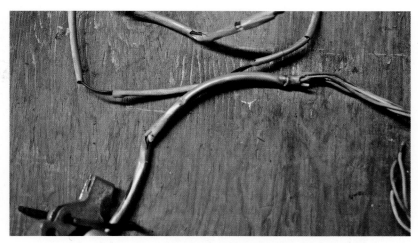

On old bikes, the sheathing for the wiring can become brittle and rotten, so it may pay either to put all-new wires up or cut the sheath off and cover with heat-shrink wrapping (HSW). If re-covering, wipe the cables clean and slide the HSW up to the switch and into the housing. Make sure all the cables are aligned before warming it up, so no wrinkling happens.

Thick rubber grips are designed to hold on to the bars, so they are going to be a tight fit. Put the new grips in a pan of very hot water to soften them up before attempting to slip them on.

old bolts, and mount the new bars in position. Sit on the bike to get them exactly right and centred. Some bars have knurled sections for the clamps to bite on – do not push them about when they are tightish, as this will score the clamps. Now put the throttle and perches or front brake on and turn the bars to and fro to check they are long enough; there will be a bit of slack on OEM but make sure the brake line or cable does not pull unduly, by lifting the front. If there is any doubt, get new cables and lines made up.

The same problems can occur with the electric cables to the switchgear, although you may get lucky and find that, with a bit of careful wiggling, there is enough slack to reach the new position.

Grips

Obviously, you will have seen a pair of handlebar grips that will look uber cool on the dream machine, but for this sacrifices must be made. Trying to get an old, hardened grip off a handlebar in

LEFT: General road grime and age will make aluminium tatty, but a quick spruce-up will transform them. Choose a good make of old lever, as the metal will be of decent quality and the design will be stylish.

BELOW LEFT: Remove the oily muck with solvent and cut off the crackly plastic knob cover before giving the lever a quick polish on the wheel.

BOTTOM LEFT: Looking good for very little effort: the new brass pivot nut is a plumbing fitment with an internal thread secured by a stainless flanged bolt at the back.

one piece is virtually impossible for a normal human, so take a sharp blade, cut along the length and peel it off. Clean up the bar and throttle tube ready for the new. This task can be hard and painful work, but it can be helped by using lubrication of a volatile nature so it evaporates off and allows the rubber to grip.

LEVERS AND SWITCHES

The choice of control levers and handlebar switches is massive, so the tips here will be based on personal preference. Obviously, they have to work and look good, so the deciding factor may be how they fit in with the rest of the bike.

Refurbishing Original or Second-Hand Parts

The mount for a lever that is not hydraulic is called a perch; it can be a separate component or integrated with switch housing. The set that comes with a bike is often the best one to use, as it means cables will fit easily and it will work with the brakes and clutch. Also, if they are on switch housing, the electrics will already be colour-coded. However, it is not rocket science to change it over. The main issue with OEM is that it is often untidily finished or has bits that will not be needed, so be mindful of the quality and consider how to neaten it up.

The first task is to clean the paint off – especially if they are old and looking a bit tatty – getting back to aluminium by whatever method works. Remove the casting marks and sharp edges using files and sanding discs, then use the polishing wheel to blend it all in. Once clean, renew the pivot pin and any bushing it may have to remove slop, then swap out all the fasteners for stainless.

loctite and stud lock

Because bikes vibrate, bits tend to come loose, so a drop of Loctite is essential for all bolted components. Studs have to be even more secure, so use a stud-lock liquid when setting them in. Clean out threads and wire-brush old bolts to remove grease and old compound before assembling.

Repainting

If they are to be repainted, all the electrical bits can come out. This is a good move, as over time contact surfaces and connections become corroded or gummed up, the wires may be frayed and plastic sleeves will be crispy and brittle. Inside the housing there will be a convoluted layout of wires, and tiny, often spring-loaded, components that can easily be lost in the mess of a shed, so care will be needed when delving into these fiddly areas.

If the idea is to repaint without disassembly, use paint thinners and a brush to wipe off the old paint, then dry thoroughly. Mask off the switches and wires and put bolts in the holes, then spray with etch primer then satin black for a classic look.

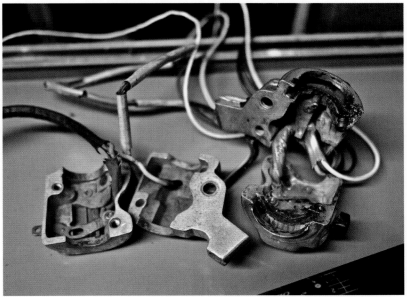

Disassembly

To disassemble a switch, take the two halves apart, noting if the wiring splits inside and how it exits. Open the pieces out and take photos of the layout or sketch a diagram (keep it in a safe place!). If it is really grimy and the colours are hard to make out, spray some carb cleaner on it and gently wipe clean with a brush or cotton bud. Alternatively, put the whole assembly into a jar, leaving to soak in some petrol or similar (not acetone as this can discolour the plastic switches). After a while, gently blow clean – do not use an airline on high pressure as bits can be blown out. If possible, have a spare to cannibalize or for visual help when assembling.

To avoid losing tiny little parts as the released springs fire them across the workshop, it helps to take a switch apart inside a large plastic tub, to contain them.

When cleaned up, a collection of old switches from scrap bikes will give a classic look to any project. The cheap plastic switch box cost many times more than all the others, yet will not last as long or look as good.

cable archive

When you remove an old cable, do not chuck it away. Clean all the grime off and give it a quick spray with fine oil, then lube the inner so it runs freely. Put it in the bag the new cable came in, or attach a plastic label to it with the make and model it came off, coil it up and store. This ensures an emergency replacement is available at any hour. If you are travelling abroad, it may even be quicker to get one sent from home than wait for local suppliers to get one. When building bikes, acquiring an 'archive' of cables will allow you to see what fits what.

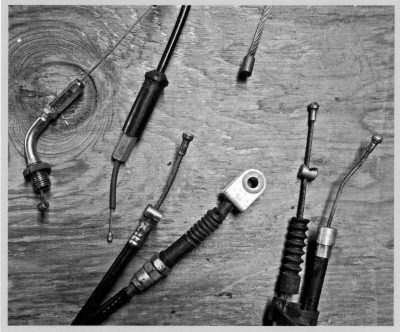

Selection of control cable end fitments. Keep these for reference when ordering and building new cables.

Rebuilding

With the housing cleaned, polished or preferably painted by powder-coating (they take a lot of flak and can get scratched easily), lay out all the parts and begin the rebuild. All contact surfaces should be shiny and proud – do not abrade too much away, as the contact area may be lost. Note the direction in which the wires to be replaced are lying. With the component securely held, melt the soldered connection with a soldering iron, pull off the old wire and immediately put the new wire on, and hold in position until it is solid. Slide the components into place over the springs (new if possible) and use Loctite on any screws. Check each circuit is working as they go in and that the wires do not crimp against the bars when put together. There may be small insulating pads inside, usually on horn and starter buttons; check their condition and make sure they go in the right way round.

CABLES

If you decide to use different bars and aftermarket carbs, and alter the frame, it is likely that the standard control cables will not fit, or will be too long.

Unless the bike has had new cables fitted recently, or the existing ones are in very good condition, replacing them should be automatic; new cables make everything work more easily, help in setting up, and look good. If the bike has been changed, do a check first to see if the original size of cable will fit; if it does, simply ordering replacements will be preferable to knocking them up in the shed. With some bikes that are commonly customized, it is possible to buy cables in different lengths. Alternatively, if you have access to a selection of cables or bikes, it may possible to find a replacement from those.

Measuring and Ordering

Parts to make up cables are readily available; send off for a catalogue and keep it in the shed so that sizes and types can be checked at source, rather than trying to work it out online. First, get a stiff electric three-core cable and use this to work out the length of the outer, by taping it to the fitment and routing it up until it reaches the control lever or throttle. Fit the tank or anything else under which it must run to the final route and use ties to secure it. Make sure it does not get kinked or stretched when the bars are turned fully in both directions. Try a couple of routes, aiming to run along the tubes in the neatest fashion.

With a vernier, size the diameter of the inner cable, outer tube and fitments needed, by measuring the original or a spare that does the same job; nipples and barrels (from now on, collectively termed 'nipples') vary in style and dimensions, so get them exact. When you have determined the sizes you need, place your order, always including an adjuster in the line, where cables split in a multiple connector box. Put the adjusters on the lower part of the cable, so that each can be individually fine-tuned. As postage is charged for these small items, it will be more cost-effective to double up on the order, to allow for mistakes and to build up the stock cupboard. Do not get fancy and try to use stainless-steel inner wire, it has to be galvanized in order to solder properly.

Longer Cables

Measure the length of the outer tube needed using a stiff length of three-core electric cable to get the curves. Check at full extension and note the measurement. If different components mean the inner may be different, place the operating end in place, including the adjusters set to middle, and measure the length from the end of the ferrule or fixed adjuster to the nipple, without the brake or clutch activated. Remove from this and put the lever end in position, including the adjuster on the perch, and, pulling in the lever, measure from the ferrule to the nipple; add these two together to get the length of the inner. The technique is the same for throttle and choke cables.

Check the size and type of end fitment and note what kind of adjusters are fixed in the cable. Do not forget to measure the bore of the cable and the inner.

Either send off to get the cable made, or knock one up in the shed if you have the fittings and raw materials. Do not use second-hand cable or inner, unless it is just for a temporary mock-up.

Cutting and Making

Cut the outer first by tightly wrapping one layer of tape around so that the cut will be made in the middle of the wrap. Grip the cable in the vice, just firmly enough to hold it without crushing, then cut near to the jaws using a fine blade on a disc cutter. A hacksaw or snips can either tear the end up or pinch the cable; it can be done with these tools, but it is tricky.

Nipples and Ferrules

One end of the inner needs to have a nipple on. Choose the end that is awkward to get to, so that the measuring for cutting is made easier by having that end out in the open near the lever.

Clean the inside of the nipple with wire wool, removing surface oxidization, to achieve a shine that will ensure that the solder takes. Now clean the end of the wire thoroughly to remove oxidization, dirt and grease, using wire wool or wet and dry paper, then wipe dry or blow with the airline. A more thorough way is to dip the end in acid – I use hydrochloric (HCl) for a count

Get all the kit ready for soldering cables. Use a heatproof block to work on and clean the nipples until they are shiny. Work slowly and calmly.

A fly-tying vice from a fishing shop is handy for holding cables and small parts while soldering.

ABOVE: Feed the solder on to the nipple, without getting it past the nipple, as this will make the wire stiff and could weaken it in heavier applications, such as on the brakes and clutch.
BELOW: The solder should form a silver mound in the nipple and fill it to the rim; if it looks black and messy, take it out and start again.

of five – to 'burn' off all the muck, and then neutralize by dipping in distilled water. Briefly dry it with a hot-air gun.

For nipples with a recess, use fine-nosed pliers to open up and bend the strands to make a small cage at the very end; this forms a plug and stops the wire slipping out of the nipple. Thread the nipple on and pull the cage in tight.

If there is no flux in the solder (electrical solder usually has it in the core), flux the inside of the nipple with a fine brush, and wire or dip the end into the flux pot. Secure the piece on to a fire-proof soldering pad or in a mini vice, to work hands-free. Heat up the nipple and wire with a soldering iron until solder fed on to it runs in, coats the whole piece and fills out the recess. Cool by dunking in water briefly, wipe clean with tissue or cloth, then give a quick buff on a soft polishing wheel. You may want to invest in a solder pot, which provides a pool of molten solder for dipping a piece. As with any soldering gear, read the instructions and be safe.

Slide the ferrules on to the outer, making sure they seat squarely, then thread the inner in and fit the end into its place. Set the outer end into the fixed hole and tape into place to stop it falling out while working at the other end. Put the adjuster in and slide the next outer on and bring it to its perch, then tape that as well. Pull the inner until it is taut and line it up with where the nipple goes, wrap a bit of tape around and mark. With very sharp snips or a fine cutting disc, cut the inner, aiming to keep the strands from flattening out. Take off and solder on the nipple.

Filling with Oil

Use a cable oiler to get some fine oil into the cable; do not use thick oil or grease, as this will clog with dirt and seize the movement up. If there is no oiler to hand, improvise a funnel at one end from card and tape or plasticine, and mount the cable hanging through the vice with the funnel at the top. Fill with oil and work the inner up and down to pull the oil through. Clean off and fit.

LEFT: The solder should form a silver mound in the nipple and fill it to the rim; if it looks black and messy, take it out and start again.

suspension, mudguards, footpegs and levers, and chain

LEFT: Classic shed builders working at Brooklands Museum, with their Doug Earle Cotton, a methanol-powered beast in a straight-tube rigid frame with girder front end. The holes are to reduce weight, a detail often seen on café racers. BELOW: One solution for a rigid frame is the weld-on hardtail on this A10 custom; the line is superb, producing a clean original bike. The cool, finned end of the oil tank looks to be a cylinder head from a two-stroke.

SUSPENSION

If all roads were billiard-table smooth, the issue of suspension would not really come under discussion, but pragmatically it is necessary to consider the bouncy bits at either end of the bike.

Suspension has two roles to play in biking: one is to smooth out bumps in the road and give a comfortable ride; the other is to keep the tyres in contact with the tarmac, thus helping the handling. When upgrading or tweaking your bike, it is handy to know what the options are and the criteria for choosing.

Rear Suspension

Rigid Frame

Looking at the back end, there is a variety of configurations available, but what usually happens is that the existing set-up will dictate what you do.

The simplest rear end is a rigid frame, which consists of the wheel being locked in the frame without being able to move. This was the earliest style of bike layout and has carried on into the

world of choppers and custom. It is known as a hardtail, with good reason, as every bump and pothole is transmitted directly to the base of the spin. Riding one of these bikes can be a pretty painful experience. Later use features on customized old bikes or frames, with the jarring effect being partly resolved

by big tyres to absorb bumps, and a sprung saddle helping the rider to stay level.

The plus side is that a hardtail can look nice and clean, and can allow low ground clearance and tyre-hugging mudguards. A number of modern Harleys have a fake up of this, which gives

the look of a hardtail, but with hidden suspension. The massive plate holding the pivot can lessen the impression of simplicity and add even more weight to a heavy bike.

Suspension Types

Early attempts at providing some suspension included the sprung hub, with the springing actually happening within the wheel, and plunger, where the axle plates were mounted on bars that moved up and down a spring-blocked tube. Neither was great, but plungers can be used to good effect, in terms of looks and some performance, with a bit of good engineering.

The most common method is to have a swing arm that is pivoted on

LEFT: My take on the plunger rear suspension, for bobber looks without the kidney-killing hardtail. With waterjet stainless parts and off-the-shelf springs rated to the correct weight, the design can be simple and effective.

BELOW: Flat-tracker monoshock set-up: these bikes take some pounding so there can be no compromise on strength. A bike with poorly designed or weak suspension is a potential death trap, so it is vital to do some research and get help.

the frame and controlled in movement by some form of shock (absorber). The set-up is quite a basic concept, with lots of room for enhancement. The two types are monoshock and twinshock – the terms are self-explanatory really. On chain drive the point of rotation is as close to the engine sprocket as possible, so any alteration in chain length, as it moves up and down, is kept to a minimum.

As is the case with all technology, shock design has come a long way from the simple jam-pot style fitted on earlier bikes. However, the developments have not necessarily found their way on to mass-produced bikes. When building a bike, most OEM tend to go for the cheapest components they can, without actually endangering the rider, and rear shocks are no exception. This has led to a massive market for aftermarket shocks, from cheap(er) pattern parts, which can actually be worse than OEM, up to hyper-expensive performance bits of kit, which use the rarest metals and finest engineering to give improved handling and ride.

How it Works

The spring on the outside is compressed with weight, so absorbs the force of any bumps (which is why it is called a 'shock absorber'). Inside, there is damping of a piston, by air/gas or oil, to slow down the process and also control the rebound. This means that shocks must be made to support the weight of the bike and average rider in average conditions for the type of bike and use. If they are too soft, the bike will give a smooth ride in gentle conditions, but will compress and wallow as the going gets harder. If the shocks are too hard, the ride can be harsh, with the back wheel hopping and losing traction; both can be dangerous, so care must be taken when replacing or choosing new.

You may notice that some are mounted with the body end at the frame and others the opposite way. Basically, the aim is to reduce the (unsprung) weight that hangs off the swing arm, so the heavy bit is mounted on the frame. This is pure physics: the greater the mass, the more momentum it has, putting extra stress on the shocks and upsetting the handling, hence the tech goal of ever lighter wheels and brake components.

Spring Compressor

The hardest part of working on shocks is getting the spring off. On a homemade jig, the hole in the top plate sits on the shock collet and, as the nuts are threaded down, it compresses the spring. Once it is down enough, lock the spring by mole grips on the shaft or jubilee clips around the coils, then let off the pressure and remove the collet; tighten up again, release the spring and let it up slowly. There is a lot of power in this, so be careful. Always clamp it securely to the bench and wear safety glasses at least.

Changing Shocks

Changing shocks is easily done, simply by supporting the wheel in position and removing the fasteners at either end. The more difficult task is deciding which shock to use.

First, they need to be the correct length to fit. If they are to be longer or shorter than stock, make sure that the chain is unobstructed along the top run and that the wheel is not going to rub on the frame or mudguard. Longer shocks will push the back end up, decreasing the rake angle of the forks and putting more weight on them, so it may be necessary to upgrade the springing in the forks. It is also important to check that the stand still reaches the ground!

Shorter will bring the back end down and the wheel closer to the mudguard or frame, possibly reducing ground clearance when cornering, as the exhaust and footpegs get closer to the ground.

Old-school shocks or OEM tend to be chromed and/or painted, usually quite lightly, so they are quick to get grubby and rusty. If you want to use them again, you should be aware that a rebuild that includes new paint and perhaps rechroming (if you like shiny) may cost more than buying a halfway decent aftermarket shock. It is of course a matter of choice. If you are going to rebuild, it is probably best to buy replacement springs or get the old ones shot-blasted and powder-coated. The body and eyes should be done the same way, ensuring any friction surfaces are masked up.

Try not to buy second-hand shocks without some knowledge of what the

Converting monoshock to twinshock: the single shock is used to set the position and height, and then the mounts for the twinshocks are made and welded in place. Afterwards, all traces of the mono set-up can be removed.

The finished conversion.

appropriate condition should be – spring length, compression needed and damping. If possible, find a decent pair to compare them with. Check for oil on the centre rod, which indicates a seal gone, mushy springs that have lost the will to bounce, and uneven compression force, then make your decision.

There are some lovely-looking shocks around, especially those with aluminium reservoirs and bodies. Do not be afraid to experiment – they can be adapted with stronger springs if possible.

Alternatively, calculate the weight of you and the bike together, then phone technical support at a manufacturer, tell them what type of riding you plan to do and ask them to suggest what would suit. From huge company to one-man band, most manufacturers will respond in a friendly and helpful way, even to daft questions – as long as you have the right attitude, listen, take notes and compare.

Once the shock has been found, it needs to be fitted, so the bolt holes in the eyes must be the correct size. If they are not, there are different sizes of metal tube for the eye available, or turn

one up from stainless or quality aluminium. Standard versions are usually plated steel and prone to corrosion. Remember to change the rubber bush in which it is set as well. Loosely bolt them in at

the top, then lift the swing arm up and slide over the studs or poke the bolts through and thread in (Loctite!). Washers should not touch the eye of the shock; they are used to lock the rubber

Changing the shock mount tube: the tube through which the bolt attaches to the frame or swing arm can be changed by positioning a socket large enough for it to slide into on one side and a smaller socket that just makes contact with the tube on the other. Put in a vice and the tube is pushed out.

Well-used Knucklehead sporting springer forks, which were the OEM for this bike – as the unsophisticated design shows. Modern repro versions are widely available and on the right bike they can work well.

and metal centre in place. After making sure everything lines up without stress, you can tighten up.

Front Suspension

Conventional Types

The evolution of bikes has been fairly limited at the front end for mainstream production, using just three types: girder, springer and telescopic. Other types have been used here and there – including leading link and single-sided hub steer – but these three are the conventional ones.

Girders are basically two arms pivoted at the headstock where the shock is also mounted, and are very simple in design. They work well, with the right shock absorber, and many variations have come about, although these tend to be custom-built and not available over the counter. Their downside is that they do not really look good on a bike – unless there is a desire to look a bit weird, which is always a possibility.

Springers on the other hand can look really good, adding a retro look to bobbers and the more laid-back bikes, such as choppers. They work with suspension units at the top and the pivot behind the wheels; the rear rods are fixed and the front ones carry the forces up to the shocks. Widely available, and used on some production 'custom' bikes, they, like all aftermarket parts, can be budget or high-end expensive, with quality and looks shadowing that graph line.

Using the same principles as rear shocks, but with internal springs and damping system, telescopic front forks are everywhere. There are good reasons for this: they are easy to set up and maintain, they look good and they do the job well.

Changing Forks

Changing out a pair of forks is a simple procedure; the main issue is making sure the new forks fit. First, measure the distance from the top of the yoke to the spindle, to get the length when using original wheels and keeping the same ground clearance. Be prepared to make brake adaptor plates and mudguard mounts, unless these come with the package. You will also need yokes that fit and possibly the steering-head spindles and bearings will need changing as well.

The new forks need to be capable of supporting the bike and rider, and give

LEFT: A lovely mash-up of periods, this Triumph flat-tracker has leading link forks. These are basically a front swing arm and with that in mind it is not hard to envision a modern take using performance shocks and clean design.

BELOW: Stanchions tightly gripped by the yoke clamps are difficult to move. Remove the bolt and put a flat bit of metal into the slot, put the bolt into the threaded section of the clamp and tighten it against the plate to slightly expand the clamp.

decent suspension. The simplest way to ensure this is to buy forks for a bike of similar weight and size; never get forks from a smaller-capacity bike unless they are going to be upgraded. Go on a forum and ask what others have used before and whether it is possible to add upgrades, such as progressive springs that slow down the dive and improve handling. It is not possible here to cover all the physics and mechanical issues involved in upgrading forks, which will be different for every bike, but understanding sizing and fitment issues is a good start.

Basically, the fork leg is a stanchion that fits into the bottom slider; it is clamped at the top in the yokes and locked on the wheel spindle. For extra rigidity, there may be a fork brace or mudguard at the top of the slider.

Inverted forks have the stanchion at the bottom with brake and spindle mounts attached. The process is the same, except the yokes will be larger, to take the sliders.

Using a wheel, even if it is only a hub, that fits the fork legs is a good start, as this means the brake mounts and spindle are all set up to work together. If the wheel and tyre are to be original or close, then the yokes can be used as well; or, if the stanchions are the same size as the ones on the bike, and you are happy to use them, then that is an

option. There are online charts that give the stanchion diameter for most bikes and these can helpful when deciding. This is the simplest fork change, as one slides out and the other slides in, with no changes to the components needed.

Swapping the Yokes

The next level is a complete front-end swap that includes the yokes as well. The problem area will be the steering head, as the spindles will probably differ in length and/or diameter. Some spindles can be easily removed from the bottom yoke by undoing the bottom clamp and driving it out with a soft hammer; this means the (original) spindle can be swapped over if it fits the new yokes. If it means boring the hole larger, get this done by a good machinist, as the fit and position are crucial. If the hole is too big, it could be possible to bore it out larger, insert a plug (welded in place) and rebore to the correct size.

If the new yokes and spindle will fit, it may be necessary to change the bearings to match; use tapered rolling sets

ABOVE: *Classic Honda single at the centre of some modern improvements, with a single-sided swing arm, mag wheels, wavy discs and USD forks. The indents in the tank give character but also increase the steering rotation without the top yoke bashing the tank.*

RIGHT: *Interesting shed design and build on a steampunk chop.*

and ensure all fits well, including oil seals and dust caps.

If the front wheel is to be wider than standard, or the differing components will not match up without serious work, then it may be a good idea to get some new yokes, either off the shelf or made to measure. Many bike engineers will make up yokes to fit different applications; these will be from good-quality aluminium and look much nicer than standard. One good method is to knock up a design and get the blanks cut by waterjet, have a machine shop carry out the precision work, then polish or paint.

Simply, a yoke is a triangular plate with three holes for the stanchions and spindle to be clamped in securely. Set out a line for the stanchions and

preventing seized threads

Some parts of a bike, such as spark plugs and exhaust rings/studs, will, depending on size and range of temperature, be prone to locking up solid. This can be prevented by using a smear of copper grease before assembling.

mark their centres at the required distance – from the original centre distance add the extra width of the tyre.

Bisect this line and measure back to the spindle hole the same distance as on the original, if using forks with the

LEFT: Trying out custom yokes, waterjet-cut in 30mm aluminium and then sent to a machine shop to remove the waste and tidy up, rather than being left as 'slab' yokes. The marks are shadows from milling and are easily polished out. The total cost is still less than off-the-shelf custom yokes and the result is much lovelier.

BELOW: Dimensioned drawing for wider yokes, sent off to the waterjet cutters.

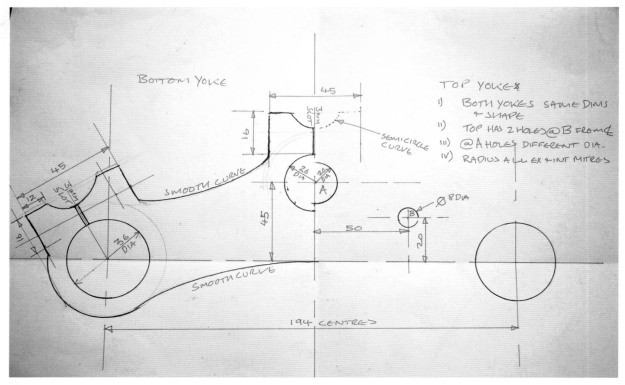

axle in the same place, and closer in if a leading axle is used; this keeps the trail and length roughly the same as the original, and should not disturb the handling too much. With these centres in, draw the holes and then make up the outer lines of the yoke, including blocks to put in the clamp bolts. Draw in slots through the clamp blocks to allow the metal to pull in and grip.

On the top yoke, mark the centres for the handlebar clamps, making sure that when all is assembled there is clearance around all the parts. Add all the dimensions and any notes to the drawing and pass this on to the waterjet cutters. If they need it in CAD format, get it converted to the correct file type.

Using Second-Hand Forks

Before using any second-hand forks, empty them of oil by removing the drain screw and squeezing over a container. After this, strip them down completely, taking photos of the disassembly to make sure it all goes back in the right order. Inspect the stanchions for wear that will make them slack, and degraded chrome that will wear out oil seals or go rusty. Check all bearing/sliding surfaces are sound and not sloppy; degrease the slider inner, springs and damping cartridge, then clean thoroughly.

Replace the O-rings, oil seals and any worn bushes, and swap out bolts for stainless, with new copper seal washers. Carry out any cleaning up of the sliders, such as removing lugs, casting marks and unneeded bits, by grinding or machining and polishing. Get them painted if desired and then rebuild.

Reassemble the front end using Loctite on all the clamping bolts and fill with the correct amount of appropriate fork oil.

Make sure the wheel is absolutely central in the forks; turn up some spacers to secure this. Set up the brakes so that there is no binding and the wheel spins freely.

MUDGUARDS

Protection from the elements is often low on the wish list of someone choosing to ride a bike, and mudguards are often hacked up or even removed. However, mudguards are not there just to look pretty – they actually have a job to do and ditching them is a personal choice. It does give the bike a certain

'rawness' when wheels and tyres can be seen unfettered, but, as soon as the rain starts, water, mud or wet gravel is encountered, flicked up in the air ending up covering the bike with grime while a broad strip of wet goo is directed directly onto the rider, front and back.

When deciding on mudguards, get a suitably shaped example and measure how long it should be. They come in two profiles: 'C' fits close to most tyre profiles, while 'D' is flatter, with distinctive sides. Once you have measured how long it needs to be, use an old tyre secured to

a block, or similar, and rest the mudguard on it while marking and cutting.

Mask the area to be cut, mark the centre line of the mudguard and measure the distance to the edge. Get some flexible material – for example, lino tiles – and cut a piece the same width as the guard. Fold it in half and then draw a decent curve that, opened out, gives a smooth shape. Mark the centre line and place on the 'guard, then scribe around.

Use a fine disc on the cutter to cut to the line as close as possible; using a small half-worn disc the curve is easier

LEFT: *Mudguards are useful if you live in a damp country and they can also look good. The close-fitting mudguard on my Sportster works really well, but some may wish for something a bit smaller.*
ABOVE: *Finding the centre line allows a symmetrical curve to be marked on; it is easier to make a line on the masking tape than on metal.*
BELOW LEFT: *The mudguard is resting on an old tyre, allowing cutting with no wobbling.*
BELOW RIGHT: *A good polish is the last job.*

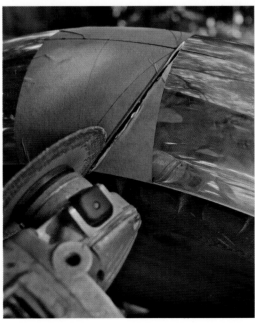

LEFT: A hand-change gear lever used to be the norm, and some people still put them on their bikes, but there is a reason why they are not standard any more. Could it be the other part of the set-up, the 'suicide clutch'? The forward controls on a 45 Harley result in the famous 'knees in the breeze' riding position.*

to follow. Do not use snips, as the thin metal will distort and buckle. With a sanding disc, shape the curve to a smooth run. If you mess up, reapply the stencil and go again; trying to adjust the overcut will result in a bad shape. Gently deburr the edges without thinning the metal, then use hand files or emery to round the edge.

FOOTPEGS AND LEVERS

Foot controls come in three configurations: rearsets, mid-mounts and forward controls. The terms are self-explanatory and the choice of configuration depends on what the bike is for and personal taste. Riding position is dictated by the position of the feet and the type of bar used, so it makes sense to get these sorted at the start of a build. The logical preference is for comfort and ease of use, but there are some extreme examples around. Whatever foot controls are chosen, they must be solidly mounted and allow the levers to do their job without hindrance.

RIGHT: Off-the-shelf universal rearsets are widely available and, with a bit of savvy, can be used in any position. Remember that frames come with mounts for footpegs and you will need to think carefully beforehand about how much work will be needed to change them or adapt the new ones to fit.

BELOW: Getting close to the limits of usability, it will be almost impossible in this set-up to get any leverage on the brake, due to the position of the peg, the length and design of the brake lever, and the location of the pivot. For safety's sake, a more functional approach is recommended.

The location of the footpegs plays a significant part in the setting out of the stance and the riding position of the bike. Fix the seat (or a cushion of the same height), the handlebars and the tank, and secure or block up the bike so it will not fall over; if there is a centre stand, use it. Get a friend to put a bar in the approximate position of the footpeg, try to get it solid, then put your foot on it. Grip the bars and sit as if you are riding. If that is comfortable, press down with the toes to see if you can work the levers. Make a note of the optimum position of the gear lever and the brake pedal, and the range of movement, so there will be enough leverage to shift gear and the brake pedal is able to apply enough movement to actuate.

The connections for levers should move freely. A bolt through two bars might seem fine until a sideways force causes it to wear oval. Where bars are on pivot points, turn up a sleeve and weld to the lever, to give lateral strength. If possible, a bush or bearing should be housed in it.

If you need to relocate footpegs and controls, either to the front of the engine as forward controls for a bobber, or further back than standard as rearsets on a café racer, then the gear and brake levers cannot be used normally. The situation will call for some mechanical shenanigans, to ensure that everything works as it should. Do not simply attach the pegs to a new part of the bike without thinking through how the gears and brake will be operated. If you are not prepared to do some work, other than attaching shop-bought kit, it is better to leave them be. It will be necessary, unless they come with all the levers in place, to mount new ones, so consider first that they could use the peg mounts as the pivot point; this is the simplest option to go for, but it will still need a bit of thought to get it right. Cheap rubbish options will have the peg on a bolt and a shaped lever, usually made from a bit of plate, rotating around it. This can cause all sorts of trouble as it can flex, or you can discover, usually under stress, that the leverage has not been worked out correctly; this means danger when you least need it. Biking should be exciting, but only in the right places.

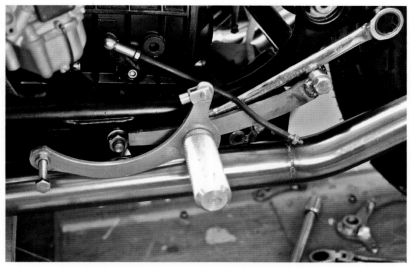

Spend time at this stage constructing a mock-up from scrap, checking the length and position of the levers so that they move the correct distance. Do not worry about looks until you are sure it all works, then get the final mechanism made, adapted and fitted. This design looked good, but it did not work well with the riding position, so further design work was needed.

The dimensions needed to make the set-up were taken from the mock-up and tidied up and then the parts were cut by waterjet in stainless.

The final set-up, all welded neatly, with rubber covers made from Jackhammer handlebar grips to match the bars, with matching shift rubber. A bronze bush inside the lever pivot ensures years of life.

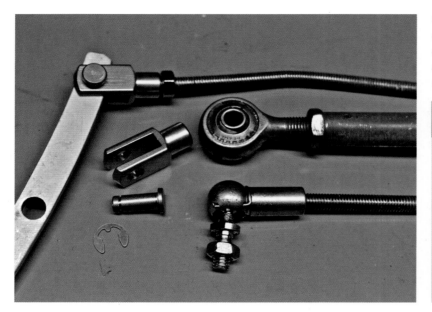

Connections for levers, clevis, rose and ball joints are all designed for this type of application and come in a variety of metals and sizes; there are many suppliers online. These either thread in (male) or fix on a threaded bar (female).

grease nipples

Pivot points, such as swing-arm spindles and brake-lever mounts, will gradually lose lubrication on the bearing surfaces; to alleviate this, install bleed nipples when fabricating them. These come in a range of sizes and length of thread; use logic to choose a suitable one. Mount in a place that is accessible when the bike is built and ensure that there are routes for the grease to get to the bearing.

CHAIN

The engine has been rebuilt and is pumping out more horses than a cavalry charge; the bike has a set of boots that would stick to an iced-up mirror; now, all that is necessary is for this power to be put on the road. What better way to do it than with a flimsy rod of metal a couple of times thicker than a watch bar. (This is a rhetorical question, so no question mark!) The chain is, unless you are playing with shafts, one of the most important components of a bike, and as such needs to be working at its optimum level at all times. If it is not, the consequences can be devastating: poor acceleration, excessive wear and eventually failure that could leave you or the bike ruined.

When putting a bike together, it is essential to ensure that the chain, which often goes on last, should be running true and taut, and that means setting it up right. In practical terms, the chain is essentially a thin articulated ladder whose rungs catch behind a shaped tooth rotating with the engine, while halfway along the same happens at the rear sprocket, creating enough energy to turn the wheel and shunt the bike and rider along. All this force is transmitted on to tiny rollers on tiny bars, joined together with strips of plate a couple of mill thick, at some-times hair-raising speeds. It is sobering to watch a slow-motion film of a chain during acceleration; it flexes from side to side and undulates with more waves

Burnt-out Brough Superior with two exposed chains: primary from engine to gearbox and final drive from gearbox. This is known as pre-unit construction and doubles the task of setting up in a new frame.

XR flat-tracker puts out about 80 horsepower, transmitted through the chain.

than a spring break off Hawaii. The idea of a tensed straight line from front to back is completely unrealistic. This component goes through hell to do its job, so it is only right that you should take care of it properly.

Set-Up

An untouched bike comes from the factory with the chain and sprockets set up true and at the correct tension. If it is well looked after, this set-up will endure for a good time to be had by all. However, when you start messing about with different wheels (this includes altering the tyre width), swing arms and frames, life gets more complicated.

With the engine in the frame, chock the bike up so the back wheel is able to rotate – assuming this is a new set-up, do not put any spacers in – and there is room to get around the back end. Check the front sprocket is vertically true (perpendicular to the floor or workbench), using a square. Measure in to the top and bottom of the sprocket

and wedge up the frame until both are exactly equal. Roughly line up the rear sprocket and do the same. If this is out, you have problems that could be down to the swing arm and it may be necessary to think about the frame set-up.

Get hold of a dead-straight bar and clamp it to the front sprocket, so that it is

flat along the surface and projects past the rear sprocket. Now slide the wheel up until the sprocket is flat against the bar and clamp it in place. To check the bar is straight, put it on a flat surface and draw a line along the length. Turn the bar over and set it on the line, then draw another line; they should match

Checking with a builder's straight edge that the sprockets line up on their flats.

up exactly. A handy alternative is a builder's square, which is made of aluminium and dead straight, and has a large side that ensures that the sprockets can be clamped true. Occasionally in scrap bins, they chuck out lengths of square section aluminium tube, which is perfect for lining up and clamping to – pay if you have to, but get it.

If the tyre size is substantially increased, the chain might be passing through the tyre or, when the tyre is centred, it could come out further than the gearbox sprocket. In either case, some engineering will need to be done.

New Sprockets

Sprockets are important parts of the drive train, so you will need to give them some serious consideration before altering. The front sprocket will be hardened steel with a spline fitting on the centre, which makes them very difficult to alter. Some manufacturers have a range with dished centres that set the sprocket out further, which can help with the wider tyre problem. If your bike does not have the option, it is possible to space the sprocket further out along the shaft, but this is only viable if the (sprocket) splines are fully mounted on the shaft splines and the nut can be tightened up fully. If not, then an expensive replacement will need to be made by a qualified engineering works. For very minor adjustment – say, a couple of millimetres – it is entirely possible to shift the engine sideways slightly, but this will require some serious planning at the framework stage.

Rear sprockets can be bought as blanks to be machined and drilled to fit. There are dished options as well, so it should not be too difficult to get hold of something that will fit. You will need the following information: number of teeth, size of chain, position and size of fixing holes, and size of centre hole needed. The last two need to be very accurate and may require a vernier and some basic geometry skills.

Sprockets are crucial on a bike – if they are in poor condition you will not be going anywhere safely. While it is easy enough to see if the rear one is shot, the front one is smaller, and hidden away under a casing. Wear such as this would result in the chain jumping and possibly jamming up.

Engineering as art: Speed Weevil has a changeover set-up to get the drive to the other side of the bike. It is set off nicely by the skateboard wheel chain tensioner.

tanks and seats

CHANGING OUT A TANK

Getting the right look for a bike often involves changing the petrol tank completely, rather than carrying out a simple paint job. The shape of the fuel tank adds a lot to the style of a bike, so it is obviously an important step to take, but not all tanks fit all bikes.

If you have found the tank for you, you will need to check it is the tank for the frame, or that it can be made to fit with a minimal amount of work. This may involve putting new tabs on to the frame and other metalwork; it is best to set up the tank on the cleaned frame before any paint goes on. Make tabs from mild steel, do all the drilling, shaping and cleaning of edges on the bench, then bolt on to the tank bracket using correct spacers; it is always a good idea to place a compressed rubber washer between the two tabs, to even out pressure and reduce vibration. Position and hold the tank in place by using sponge packers and gaffer tape.

Finding the right position

If possible, use existing mounting points either on the tank or frame to save doing things twice, or cut brackets off the tank if they are definitely in the wrong place or in the way. Place the tank in position on the frame. If the engine is out, make sure there is clearance for the head and that any electrics such as the coil are in place, unless they are to be relocated. Centre it and get it level so the fuel outlet is at the lowest point – remember, a tap needs to go on here, so do not make it too tight to the engine or frame.

If the tank sits higher, one method involves rolling card over the top tube to form a tunnel, then spraying release oil on this and the underside of the tank, wedging it into position and filling the gap with expanding foam. This will give the shape for the new tunnel, which is handy if the fabrication takes place away from the bike.

Real eye candy: although it is not really practical or usable, this old two-stroke custom, more a bicycle than a bike, is beautiful in its simplicity. It is a joy to check out the details.

To get an idea of what shape and size tank will go with the bike, find a side image of a (potential) tank and the length, and then draw a scaled outline on card or plastic to get the template.

Mocking up the lines of the bike will show how everything works together, and enable you to gauge dimensions such as the shock length. All the parts are grubby but this is not an issue at this stage; there is no need to waste time cleaning up components that will not be used.

Aluminium shell that is similar to the tank – try to use what is available for inspiration. A seat base and an experimental bit of bodywork allow the format to take shape. Cross-brace tubes have been removed and another pair fixed to the lines of the battery box – it is important to strengthen about the area if you are removing or changing a frame layout.

For mounts, get one half fixed in position, then use a board template to make and match up the other half.

For a tank that fits on but does not quite match up, try getting very firm foam, cut it to shape to provide support and then strap the tank on. Do not use polystyrene or similar, as they are soluble in petrol.

Centre it by a line drawn on a strip of masking tape along the centre. This can line up with a cord dropped through the headstock or wrapped around the top nut, which is pulled to a centre at the back of the bike. Get this right or it will annoy you every time you look at it.

safety

Only when there is no doubt that all flammable material and vapour has been removed can a tank be worked on. **DO NOT** attempt to cut open a tank with a disc cutter prior to this, as the sparks from the blade can set off an explosion.

Tack the tabs in place on the frame, but be aware that there could be petrol fumes about, so take proper precautions. If in doubt, always de-gas the tank.

If the standard tank is not that lovely and another one you like does not fit, do not bin it. It can be made to work, depending of course on how far you want to take it.

De-Gassing

The most important issue is that the tank must be completely leak-proof, so some form of welding will be necessary if it is going to be cut about. Obviously, the idea of heating up metal enough to melt it, or creating lots of sparks while cutting away parts, has to be tempered with an awareness of the explosive nature of petrol. Unless the tank has been open to the elements for a very long time, which can bring its own problems of corrosion inside, there is a chance that some residual vapour could be present. It is not enough simply to empty it and leave the top off for a while; if that method does not work properly, the outcome could be fatal.

Before any physical work is carried out, a tank must be de-gassed, removing all traces of petrol vapour. To do this, spray degreaser inside and then fill with water and wash out, fill again and leave for a couple of days.

A pressurized steam cleaner blown in will get rid of residue and fumes as well.

The belt and braces way is to do the above, then put a tube into the tank from the exhaust of a vehicle and leave it running for an hour or so.

Getting Rust Out

It may look possible to get a sand-blasting nozzle in and spray around, but this is only effective if you can get every bit of abrasive out. Any fine grit will play havoc with your engine should it get into the system. Get a big handful of nuts about M8 size, pour into the tank and start shaking it all about, agitating it as much as you can, to dislodge the corrosion. After emptying all the big stuff out, attach a tube to the end of an airline and blow it all clean, then wash out with some good swirls of warm soapy water.

This is a good method to start with – energetic and noisy – but it does leave a lot of rubbish in the seams and nooks.

De-gassing to remove petrol vapour by running the car exhaust into the tank. Left for about an hour, this will make the tank safe for working on with a cutter or welder.

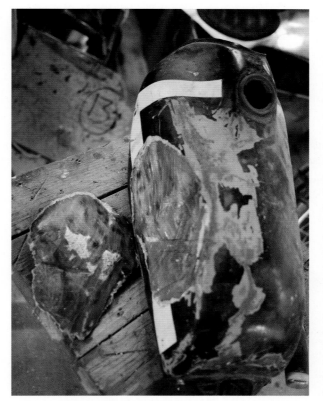

This tank (left) has become corroded inside, so will need to be cleaned before use. The dent has been covered by filler and will need to be beaten out and refilled. If any fuel (especially two-stroke) has been left in, it may end up as a hard toffee-like coating when it degrades. Taking off the fuel tap (below) should give an indication of the interior condition: rust is obvious, whereas a brown-coloured coating indicates old fuel.

To get fuel residue and other gunge out, put the old tap on and have the filler cap ready. Wear safety gear – eye protection, gloves, and so on – and have a solid base to rest the tank on, outside, away from pets, kids and nice garden bits. Have a bucket of clean water to hand in case you get splashed by chemicals and deal with any accident immediately as they are corrosive to human skin.

Fill the tank to a couple of inches from the top with water and then pour in about 500g of caustic soda – NOT the other way round, as this could cause an explosion! Top up with water, seal and leave to stand for a couple of hours. Swirl the tank a bit and carefully let off any pressure, then seal again and leave for a day or two. Dispose of this liquid, following the manufacturer's directions. Note how horribly coloured it is, with rust, petrol residue and old tank sealant. Flush out a couple of times with a hose and clean water.

Deep Clean

Even after the second method, there will probably still be rust and gunge in the tank. Seal it again, pour in about a litre of water and then add about 250g of Spirits of Salt (strong hydrochloric acid used for cleaning toilets of limescale). ALWAYS add to the water and not the other way around. It will fume a bit so let out the pressure, then seal, taking care not to inhale any of the fumes. Next, roll the tank over and around for about five minutes to get the acid into all the seams, and then leave for twenty minutes. Have a look inside and note the effect it is having on the metal. If you feel it is necessary, add some more acid and repeat until the metal is like new – the effect should be that dramatic!

Dispose of the liquid properly and hose out the tank to stop the acid burning more metal away. A drop of bleach mixed in will neutralize the acid.

This is all that needs to be done, apart from drying the tank quickly to prevent it rusting again. Take off the tap and the cap, use a hot air blower to warm up the inside and evaporate the water out. This should not take long, so do not overdo it, as this could cause the metal to buckle.

Etching and Protecting

If you really want to go the whole hog, after the clean use a suitable tank-lining material, or purge with phosphoric acid – just for a couple of minutes – and then give it a quick rinse out. The acid is weak and as a reducing agent it will stabilize and convert the surface (which is always oxidizing) to a more stable compound.

CHANGING THE TUNNEL

Welding a petrol tank up is a serious affair. Unless you have the kit and the skills, the job should be taken to someone who is better able to do it properly. It is, however, possible to carry out the donkey work at home, just using the welding shop when everything is ready. The underside of a petrol tank (known as the tunnel) is an ideal place for a manufacturer to hide components, so many tunnels are very complicated in terms of their shape. Obviously, changing the location of coils or other items, cleaning up tubes and installing a new seat can mean that the original pattern will no longer fit, so putting the original tank tunnel on to the chosen tank may not be an option. If a new tunnel needs to be made up, it can be done either in one piece or in sections.

Using the original tunnel on the new tank may seem the easiest option on paper, but in reality it can be a headache to achieve. It usually demands too much fiddly work, so it is not worth taking this route unless – and this will be down to your confidence – there is a good match, the metal is up to being aggressively cleaned and welded, or you simply want the challenge or the experience.

Cutting out the bottom of the new tank is best done with a fine disc blade. Marking out the area to go with tape will allow you to make adjustments until everything is sharp and symmetrical. Make a shelf or rim all the way round, so the new piece will have something to rest against; butt-jointed welds in thin metal are difficult and any leaks will be hard to rectify later when fuel has been put in. If there are tight corners where the disc cannot reach, cut near to the line and then use a disc or tin snips to cut straight lines into the area, reducing it to a collection of strips that can be snipped off easily. Clean all

cleaning a tank by science

Get a cork or make a rubber bung that fits the filler spout and fix a steel rod projecting into the tank through the centre; do not let it touch the metal of the tank. Mix 200g of baking soda (sodium bicarbonate) in water and fill the tank. Put in the bung and attach the rod to the positive cable of a battery charger. Earth the tank to the negative and turn on. Leave for a good few hours, then empty. The tank should be clear of rust.

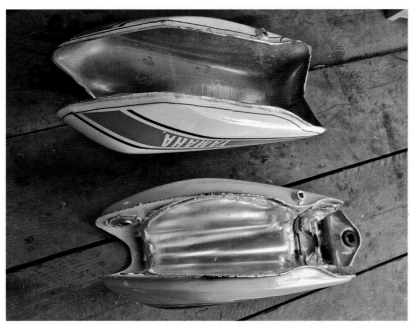

Tunnel changing on alloy tanks: one has a new tunnel and the other has been cut out ready.

ABOVE: *Steel tanks with cut-out put in. Welding steel is less specialized and cheaper to do. Cutting out the bottom means blasting can clean the interior more easily.*

LEFT: *Using masking tape to get the height of the tunnel for a replacement tank or to rework the old one.*

BELOW: *Cutting out the shape to the front of the aluminium replacement to sit correctly using the information from the mock-up.*

the rim of burrs and sharp edges, but do not thin the metal too much as it needs to take a weld. With a critical eye, look at the rim and make sure any convolutions have been flattened to simplify the new metal fitting against it.

Fold board over the spine to create a mock-up of the tunnel projecting lower than the tank, and secure well. Put the tank into place and securely wedge in the correct position. Mark both sides of the (tunnel) board by tracing

the bottom seam of the tank; do not worry too much at this stage about perfection as it will be smoothed out in production. Take everything off and refine the drawn line to give a straight line along the tunnel, evening out any

ABOVE: A stop has been tacked to the tank to show the height of the new tunnel before cutting out the old.

ABOVE RIGHT: Cut out leaving a flange to rest on. The toffee-coloured gloop stuck to the inner is old fuel residue and needs dissolving to get off.

RIGHT: The new tunnel has been roughly shaped and is tacked in place, allowing the seams to be dressed down for a neat fit.

LEFT: Shaping sheet metal is made a lot easier with the English wheel, which can roll in curves and pull metal around. This is a serious industrial model. Smaller, cheaper models are available and keep their resale value well.

softening aluminium

To soften (anneal) aluminium so that it can be worked or bent, gently heat it with a blowtorch. Colour the area to be heated with a magic marker – when the marking disappears, the metal will be annealed.

undulations and getting both edges on the same plane. Cut out the result.

Next, make a board template that covers the hole in the tank, carrying the shape up the front as needed. Mark the centre and set out where the tunnel shape will sit, and then cut it in half. Place the edges of the tunnel template on their lines on the base templates and attach with gaffer tape. It now needs to be laid out flat to give a complete template for the undersides, so the front upstand may need to be left undone for now. Look at the result and figure out if it will be possible to make it in one piece or whether smaller pieces, cut and put together, would be easier. If in doubt, go for the sectional route, as any mistakes will not use up so much metal or affect the whole. When using sections, always allow a flange to overlap the joint and make welding easier.

Blending

Find a suitable length of fixed bar the diameter of the spine, possibly a handrail, or set up a tube across a gap and clamp the tunnel metal with the centre line running along the top, and pull the sheet around. Use a rubber mallet to take it closer to the curve; if necessary, put it sideways on a flat surface to beat down and complete the fold.

Now, put a flange on the bottom sheet by beating across a straight edge. If the flange has to follow an angle, cut small vees out so that it does not crumple on the corner. To get a perfect right-angled flange, clamp the sheet between two flat bars, with the proposed corner line running level with their top, and hammer it over. For a radiused corner on the flange, use a length of wood that has had the corner filed and sanded down to the desired shape.

The process of sheet shaping in a shed is one that depends on the kit available; it will boil down to whatever you can make use of. I haven't bought anything more complicated than a small panel-beaters hammer set for the work I do; fire-extinguishers, table edges, vice jaws and homemade plywood forms have all been used amongst others. So experiment.

To assemble the sections, use plenty of gaffer tape, leaving clear sections for tacking, or use one or two pop-rivets to pin them together; the rivet holes can be sealed later during welding. Attach the tunnel to the tank and tape or tack everything together once it is all sitting correctly, then take it to the welder.

THE SEAT

Making a seat for a bike is not that difficult – at least, making the base and cushioning is fairly easy. It is possible to do the covering too, but there are plenty of upholsterers around who can do the job at what seems a reasonable cost, considering the work involved.

GRP-Based Frame Seat

With the tank in position, along with any other components that affect the seat, work out the plan shape of the seat, following the lines of the frame rails and blending it nicely into the tank. Make a cardboard template of one half, then transfer this to hardboard, turning it over to complete symmetrically. Cut out the shape and rub the edges clean.

Old Rickman Métisse flyer showing the variations possible using their different tank, seat and other components on the same basic frame. Rickman frames are still available to order. They are meticulously well made and finished, with different mounting configurations for various popular engines. Considering it is a world-famous design, the cost is not excessive.

A shed-built seat gives you an accessory that suits your bike, not somebody else's, which will fit better and look good for less than a shop-bought item. Ribbed seats and real leather look great. Shop-bought ones are usually vinyl-covered, which may be better in the wet but can look a bit plasticky.

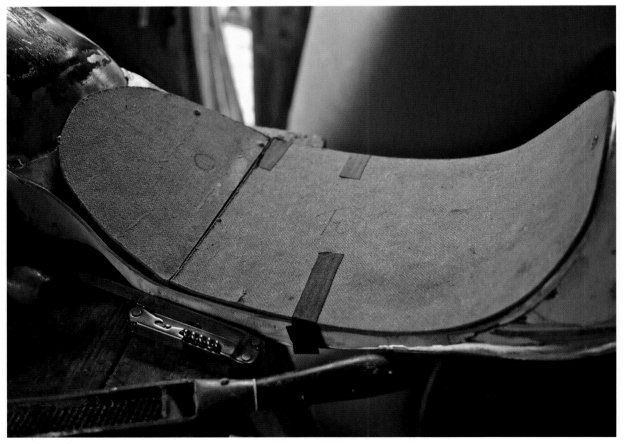

Hardboard shaped and taped in place.

If there are any projections under the seat, cut out enough for the template to sit in place, and tape a cardboard cover over the projection. Now cover any exposed material around the seat with packaging tape and aluminium foil, to prevent damage from any spilt resin. Position the template securely so it curves around and follows the lines; if it needs to be contoured, warm it up with a hot air gun to soften the glue, then press and secure into place.

Now is the time to put in locators for the mounting bolts. Drill through the template and place a greased bolt up through. Thread a nut down to a position where it will be locked into the GRP and grease any thread showing, to allow easy removal. If more rigidity is desired, a tunnel can be made, which will also allow cables to sit under the seat. Place a former on to the template – rope can be used here – and tape over to make a ridge.

Glassing

Get into protective clothing with disposable gloves; as they are quite delicate, try one pair over another. Arrange a mixing pot with about a litre of polyester resin in, a measure of catalyst (MEK), disposable 50mm brush, rollers and sharp knife/scalpel on a covered bench.

Pour in the MEK and mix well with the brush or clean wooden paddle or stick. Take a piece of mat and liberally coat with resin – you do not need to work it in, as it will soak through on its own. Lay wet side down on to the template, pushing the damp mat over any mounting nuts.

Repeat with the other two sheets, then paddle-roll the whole surface until it is a uniform green, with resin spread completely throughout the mass.

Cure time depends on the temperature, but will probably be within half an hour, so keep an eye on it, as it must be trimmed before it goes brittle. The moment to trim is when a blade will slice through the edge without dragging the fibres, leaving a cleanish edge. Slice off around the edge of the base and ditch the sticky remnants.

Leave until it is hard and tack-free, then lift off and clean all mess and protection away. Take it outside, wearing mask and goggles, to do any necessary cuts or shaping with a disc cutter,

Cover the whole template with packaging tape and spray with release oil (WD40 or similar).

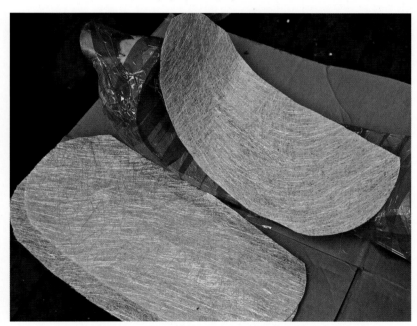

Cut three pieces of heavy (60gm) fibreglass mat just larger than the template.

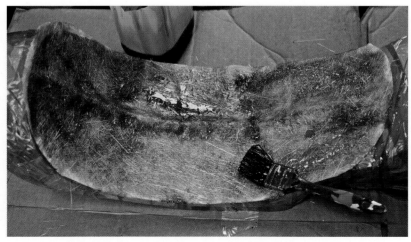

Glassing: the resin permeates throughout the mat, giving a uniform colour.

then sand the edge round to a smooth finish. The dust generated is horrible, itchy and not healthy, so make sure you clean up thoroughly.

Rather than build the locating/mounting bits in with the GRP, they can be fixed in afterwards. Drill holes through the GRP and put a nut and bolt into position through them, either way depending on the need; the bit that is staying should be dry on the outside and all threads well lubricated to prevent resin sticking to them.

Cut two rings of mat to go around the head and one patch to cap everything. Resin up the mat and put in place, rings first then cap, pushing into position with the brush. With a roller, blend into the cured GRP and let it set.

TOP LEFT: *Mat completely saturated with resin and rolled with paddle. Keep an eye on this!*
ABOVE: *Cured and trimmed base, ready to use.*

LEFT: *Place the locating pins or bolts in the holes and proceed.*

Foam

The shape of the seat, and its comfort, are dictated by the foam. There are a number of types available, including gel inserts, so it can get as complicated as you want. Choose the foam you are going to use, perhaps by cannibalizing an old seat, and place it on the base, then cut around to get the plan shape. As custom seats look better slim and organic, as opposed to the standard bloated sofa style that many modern bikes sport, the following simple method seems to produce decent results.

Level the top of the foam roughly, to follow the desired design, using a surform file or knife. Leave it higher than the finished article, so the foam will be compressed and hold its shape better.

Using decent cloth gaffer tape, start at one end and cover the foam in strips of tape; the profile of the foam can be pulled and changed by the amount of tension on the tape and its direction. To prevent a tapered/sharp edge, apply the tape in the centre first and pull down horizontally, so the foam compresses in a level fashion. As the tape is wrapped under the base, the edges will form a radius, the slope of which can be altered by tension.

Take the seat to the upholsterer and describe the finish that you want. For seats such as this, ribbing gives more character and holds the form better. A smooth covering is tricky, because if the foam overly settles, it can end up looking like a deformed slug has died on the bike. There is a type of seat known as the 'squashed baguette', which has rather taken the custom world by storm. The problem is that seats are best done in black, which works well with most styles and schemes, but not necessarily with the squashed baguette.

Sprung Saddles

The above method can also be used to make a sprung saddle, although, due to its self-supporting nature, the GRP and mountings must be top-notch. In this case, it is usually safer to make a metal base. The metal can be what you want. Just be aware that, if it needs shape, thicker plate will be hard work, although not too difficult. It is quite possible to use off-cuts of aluminium checker plate or stainless plate, for example. Unless

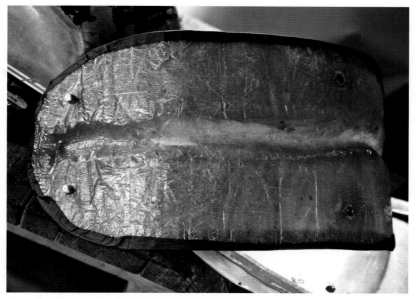

The underside with pins and protective tape around the rim of the base.

Using decent cloth gaffer tape, start at one end and cover the foam in strips of tape; the profile of the foam can be pulled and changed by the amount of tension or direction of the tape.

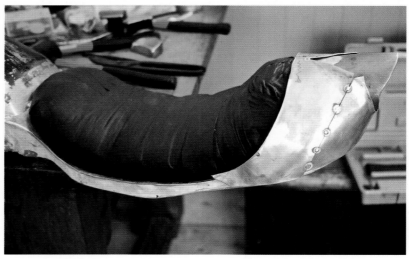

Ready for a leathering.

there is a specific reason for using a particular metal, go with what you can get.

Shape-wise, a sprung saddle is very simple. It is the size that is important and the options can range from a teeny bicycle style to a tractor seat; it all depends on the bike and your vision, so look around and get some ideas. Once again, draw a template – make it a full one, so you can get the size and proportions and to enable you to match up both sides exactly. Transfer the shape to the metal, clamp the plate to something solid and cut the shape out; do not try to do tight curves with a disc blade, as it can jam and shatter. Instead, chop it out in straight lines then work down to the curve. Smooth all the edges and make sure it is symmetrical.

While it is flat is the time to mark up and put in any holes. As the shape is fairly simple, one way to fix the seat cover is to rivet it around the perimeter. Scribe a line about 10–12mm in from the perimeter all the way round and mark off the rivet spacing (10–20mm), then centre-pop each one. Drill out to rivet size and clean off burrs.

Seat and spring mounts can be located by holes drilled in the plate and this should be done before any bending; after any further shaping, nuts or bolts can be welded in place.

Putting a curve into any plate thicker than a few mill can be hard work, and might need some lateral thinking. I have actually gone so far as to drive my truck on to a plank resting on a solid fire extinguisher that was resting on the seat, supported by two logs; it was a pain, but it worked. Metal will bend in a fairly even curve before it fails and suddenly kinks; the trick is to release the pressure before it gets to this point. If you beat it around a shaper, be aware that hammering will scar the surface, so you need to use a piece of wood to protect it, or use a non-metal mallet. Weld in any needed bits to match up with the pivot and spring set-up.

Leatherwork

To shape leather to fit, get hold of some dense hard foam, of the type used for surfboards, or anything fine enough to sand and hold its shape. Shape to fit the seat base and then, with a surform or shaping knife, form the upper shape of the final seat and tape it into place. Make sure all the edges are smoothed round, as leather could get cut and tear on sharp edges.

Take a sheet of good-quality vegetable-tanned leather about 2.5mm thick, large enough to cover and wrap the whole seat completely. Soak the leather in fairly warm water until bubbles stop rising, then put in a polythene bag and leave for a couple of hours to let the water distribute itself evenly through the hide. Make a sandbag by filling a pillowcase or cloth bag with enough fine play-pit sand that it can form and hold a dip about the size of the saddle. Put it on the floor and lay a plastic sheet over it; this will hold the seat in place without marking the leather as it is pulled around.

Put the wet hide, smooth side down, on to the sandbag and place the seat upside down in the centre. Now it gets a bit physical – the technique is to pull the leather around the seat and overlap the edge of the underside to the rivet line. This will involve grabbing the edges of the leather and pulling, possibly standing or kneeling on the seat, as much as possible, then gathering the edges together, and twisting until it is pulled to the seat. Use rope, clamps or whatever to help this and lock the leather in place as tight as you can possibly get. Once it has been secured, store it somewhere to dry out completely; this will probably take a couple of days, depending on the speed of drying.

These seats are good for inspiration; interestingly, the price of the simplest was substantially more than it cost to get the project seat covered in leather.

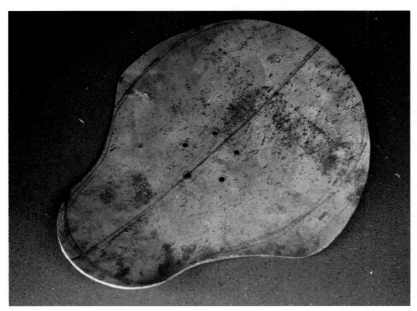

Base cut from aluminium checker plate found in a scrapyard.

RIGHT: Leather, foam and bases ready to start on seat fabrication.

BELOW RIGHT: Underside of finished bobber seat made by the stretched leather method.

BOTTOM: This minimalist seat was made by fixing stiff foam on the stainless base; a silicon laptop case with a tyre pattern on was sacrificed for the cover, soaked in hot water, pulled over and held in place with modern high-strength glue.

When it is absolutely dry, use a very sharp blade and cut the knot off, leaving a good hem over the rivet holes. It should now hold the shape to which it has been moulded and will be ready for attaching.

Shape the seat foam as before, leaving it proud so that the leather compresses it and there are no gaps; you could also go a bit fancy and put firmer foam along the centre, which will give better support and feel less like sitting on a bench. Fit the leather over and tightly tape it, allowing access to the hem. Starting in the centre of a long edge, press a drill bit into the leather, find the indent for a hole and drill through. (Do not go too deep, as this will tear the foam.) Put in a rivet and fix it. Work outwards, drilling and riveting, from this to the sharper curves; to stop pleating on the tighter curves, it may be necessary to cut small wedges from the hem to allow overlap or snugger lines.

These basics can be improved and fancied up as much as desired. It is up to you.

PROJECT: BMW STREET TRACKER

Building a bike for the streets and the open road requires a different take on customizing from creating a bar hopper or off-roader. The best examples draw inspiration from different styles to achieve a machine that is usable, fun and cool. The first step is to make a list of the major components needed and start doing some research online, or visit shops and venues for bikes to see what takes your eye. If you spot something cool on a bike, talk to the owner and ask about it; they could help you avoid a lot of legwork. This is especially relevant if it is bespoke, as, price aside, the maker can tailor your order to your needs and prevent frustration when an off-the-shelf item will not fit.

This particular project took a simple and strong bike that was wrapped in plastic body coverings and excess metal, of a somewhat lumpen

LEFT: Stripped of weight, tidied and tightened up, this BMW airhead custom is designed and built to ride.

BELOW: Seriously sensible, 1989 R100RT BMW is not a pretty bike. Underneath, however, is a lovely engine and a good basis for a modern custom.

ABOVE: Looking at the pile of unwanted dressing and bulky fitments, it is obvious that the weight lost is going to bring about an improvement in performance. This can then be built on, as the rest is improved.

RIGHT: Ready-made loops and frame mods are becoming available to builders as more bikes are built and a commercial opportunity arises, so check these out first. For the BMW, a complete loop from another bike was cleaned and fitted, giving perfect lines and good quality.

appearance, and shaped it into something lovely.

The first step was was to reduce it to its core of frame and wheels. It is acceptable to use the original tank on a Beemer like this, and people do, but it is a blocky old thing and slimming a bike is usually a good move. Obviously, retaining this massive ungainly box was a matter of taste, so there is nothing more to say.

The usual route of detabbing (culling extra metal) and adding a new rear loop was followed with the frame. A couple of extra gussets were added to the headstock to tidy up and add some more strength. It is important to pay particular attention to two of the most important structural points on a frame: where the shocks mount and at the headstock. The strengthening of these will stiffen up the frame and reduce flex, allowing harder riding and be worthy of a performance increase.

With the engine in the rolling chassis, you can start to picture the stance of the bike, thinking about the bars, tank and wheels as the major components that shape the finished machine. Riding position is a major factor here. If the bike is to be used mostly around town, sitting upright will allow better awareness of traffic, while wideish bars will facilitate controlled manoeuvring, and having the feet in line with the body will make it easier to step down at lights and junctions. Extremes of position may make a bike stand out in terms of looks, but they can also make

Mocking up the tank to see how it will look; when using old parts, you may need to use some imagination to see what they will look like when cleaned up and/or painted.

A GRP seat base fits the mock-up of the tailpiece perfectly and can be sent off for leather upholstering while the bodywork is completed. Coordinating the schedule of the longer jobs to get them started first can reduce the overall project time.

A battery box made from aluminium checker-plate allows the battery to slide in and lock. Hangers are stainless steel made from tube and old stone fixings.

riding uncomfortable or control awkward. The 'sit-up-and-beg' style is ergonomically sound and makes riding a pleasure. Grab some handlebars that are the right shape and size, stick them on and try the bike for feel. Squint at the result and try to imagine what it will all look like when it is done.

Tank

The shape of the tank will influence the seat design. The aim should be to find one that reaches along the spine and fills the space nicely from the headstock to the seat. If it slides on, all well and good. If it does not, and you feel convinced that it is the one that looks best, it can still be altered underneath to match. Wedge it into place using foam packing to get it sitting level, with the fuel tap at the lowest point. Look at how the bottom line runs; will it flow into the seat arrangement with no serious doglegs? In this case, a café-racer-style tailpiece was going to be used, not just as a visual treat but to contain electrical components so that they did not have to be mounted on the frame.

An old aluminium tank in good condition looked to fill the role here, giving the chance to do something different by concocting a one-piece tank-seat unit. The lines would be organic and the use of such a forgiving material made it possible to attempt a first shot at bodywork.

Sitting Pretty

Seat bases with a hump are widely available, so, once you have decided on whether to use GRP or aluminium, you should be able to hunt one down. Once painted, the difference in material will be largely irrelevant; it is the appearance that counts. Because it will be stamped out of sheet, the aluminium version will be a simple shape and will usually have a straight line under the seat. This will affect the line, as the seat will have to be flat-bottomed, which means it will be rather plain and possibly incongruous on a curved frame, with its swooping lines.

GRP is cast, or laid out, in a mould and can hold much more interesting shapes for less cost than metal. It is possible with GRP to build up and add material, to shape it into something that works with the style needed. The material is relatively inexpensive, but it does require some careful work to get a good finish.

Complete tank seat units in fibreglass also exist, but these are rare.

Buying a seat off the shelf is obviously a simple option and the result should, if it is made for the model of bike, fit nicely. If you buy online, however, you need to be aware that the real thing may not live up to its image and the quality of the materials may not be outstanding. Having done a bit of looking around at what is available, you may well find that having a bespoke seat made to your design will not cost much more than a run-of-the-mill shop item. There will be some work involved, but this is a satisfying process, with the added kudos at the end of having an exclusive article.

LEFT: The first design for the footpegs used knurled aluminium, with homemade levers linked to the controls. Located under the gearbox and using footpeg mounts, the battery box is hardly seen when the exhausts are in place.
BELOW: The final design for the footrests and levers was in stainless, with bronze bushes. The rear brake link was changed from rod to cable.

LEFT: A waterjet-cut and mounted fork brace also held the brake lines and mudguard in place. The standard forks are often the easiest option, as in this case, with the addition of progressive springs bought cheaply on an auction site, new bushing and seals to make it all tight. A visit to an online forum finds the best oil and the amount to use for this model.
BELOW: A simple engine stand allows a grubby engine to be cleaned easily. The sawdust is used to soak up the degreasing liquids.

Start-Up Power

Batteries have developed over the years and it is now possible to obtain compact, lightweight yet powerful units that can be mounted in any orientation. Obviously, these are pricey compared with the old-school simple wet-cell versions, so a bit of budgeting may be required. Be practical when choosing a battery. Decide what work the bike is going to be doing, and how reliable it will need to be, and then consider the extra cost of a good battery in terms of the number of years it will last without trouble. You may well come to the conclusion that the best is affordable. Obviously, a kickstart bike does not need a big battery, but it is still going to save a lot of tears if it does not pack up on you when needed.

New Boots

Much of a bike's presence relates to the way in which it is shod. The right wheels will set off the style and contribute much to the looks, so the aim is to decide what is best for your needs without compromising performance. In contrast to the old classics, the modern road bikes usually have fatter tyres on smaller rims, to improve contact and handling, but they do tend to look too small, especially with the larger-proportioned tanks and seats that pass for factory styling. Old-school wheels would be around 18-inch on the rear and 19-inch up front, which is quite skinny compared with today, but with elegant proportions – a good starting point.

Chunky tyres needed wider rims and possibly the standard fork and swing arm will not take them. This could mean more expense and work, so you need to be sure it is what you want. Obviously, if you use wheels, you will be stuck with the tyre they can take. If you use wire spokes, the hub, with all the brakes, sprockets and bearings you need, can be kept while the rim is swapped. If the standard wheels are to be used, then life gets easier, especially if they are cast and need cleaning; spoked wheels may have corroded parts, such as spokes or rim, that need to be dismantled for sprucing up.

The decision here was to build a pair of spoked wheels front and rear with the largest tyres that would fit. Allow time to hunt around for these and for suitable rims, to get the right ones at a

Sprayed with high-temperature barbecue paint, the engine is then highlighted by sanding the edge of the fins back to metal. It is simple and very effective.

good price, as well as finding someone to build them.

Hub Change

The wheels on the BMW were cast and could be considered rather ugly, so it was decided to upgrade to wire spokes, giving the bike a classic and lighter look. This was not a problem for the front, but, being shaft drive, the rear had to have a hub that fitted the bevel drive. Once again, the online forum turned up trumps, showing how to modify a spoked hub from another model to fit. After following the diagrams and tech info, the new (second-hand) hub sat in place nicely.

A spoked wheel with a hub that will fit the bike was sourced. It was cut out of the rim as these spokes, which were unwanted, are very difficult to remove.

The hub centre had to be machined to match up, then was powder-coated and rebuilt with an alloy rim and stainless spokes. Making up wheels can be a significant part of the cost of the project, so consider buying ready-made.

ABOVE LEFT: The original wheel above a second-hand wheel bought purely for the hub.
ABOVE RIGHT: Wider alloy rims in grubby but good condition were sourced from a breaker's yard, then cleaned up and made ready for lacing.
RIGHT: The finished wheel with a hubcap over the unsightly centre, turned from an old grinder housing and topped off with a 1950s car horn button.
BELOW LEFT: As wider tyres were wanted, a few modifications were made, including a slight cut-out on the shaft housing to give clearance at the back. This still needed to allow the shaft to rotate without catching.
BELOW RIGHT: The yokes were made up 10mm wider, so this old Harley alloy hub was turned with discs 5mm further out each side, allowing the standard brakes and mounts to be used. Shod with chunky rubber, it starts to look the business.

The exhaust was made from stainless tube salvaged from a milk factory scrapyard. Two variants were made; selling the unused one will recoup some of the build cost.

Instead of a speedo, a circular sat-nav was mounted in a housing machined from an aluminium fire extinguisher. This has a jack that links to in-helmet earphones.

Turning the housing.

The completed housing, showing the handlebar mounting and securing rim.

The BMW airbox is an ugly plastic box that ended up in the bin. It was replaced by this unusual aluminium shape, part of an industrial juicer, which was found in a scrapyard and given a new lease of life.

A curved tube left over from exhausts joins the airbox to the carbs. The inlet sleeves were made from bodywork sheet.

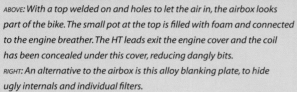

ABOVE: With a top welded on and holes to let the air in, the airbox looks part of the bike. The small pot at the top is filled with foam and connected to the engine breather. The HT leads exit the engine cover and the coil has been concealed under this cover, reducing dangly bits.

RIGHT: An alternative to the airbox is this alloy blanking plate, to hide ugly internals and individual filters.

BELOW: Finished and very photogenic, most of the custom elements were made from second-hand parts, modified in the shed. The rear light is a VW camper lens housed in the body of a WW2 mortar shell, turned and welded into the tailpiece.

Oil Cooler

The addition of an oil cooler can significantly improve life for the engine, as overheating can reduce performance substantially. An aftermarket unit originally for a pit bike was mounted on the down tubes to make the most of airflow. Upgrade the oil lines to braided with aluminium performance fittings, either ordering from the manufacturer or building your own.

LEFT: *The oil cooler was sprayed black and the edges of the fins sanded down to bare metal for contrast. The mounts are a pair of cable clips.*
BELOW LEFT: *Braided line is ordered by the metre and connections can be designed for various angles or routes.*
BOTTOM LEFT: *Attach the fittings and measure up the line length. Use a cable tie or tape to prevent fraying when cutting.*
BELOW: *Fit parts together and tighten according to instructions. Use new compressible washers to mount.*

working with metal

Gone are the days when a shed welder was the size and weight of a brick-filled tea chest. Modern inverter welders weigh as much as a large sandwich, will run all day and are easier to use, due to the flow of the current.

WELDING

Metal is joined (welded) by heating adjacent surfaces enough so that they flow together, usually adding more metal at the same time to build up the thickness and strength of the weld. It is a highly skilled process if all aspects of its application, types of metal and use of machinery are to be covered, but the shed builder should be able to get by with a modest knowledge and some basic techniques.

It is probably advisable for a recreational builder to stick to simply tacking metal into place and then getting it finished properly by a qualified welder. Obviously, with more practice taken and improved skills, you may feel you can take on the whole job. Just be aware that, when a weld fails on a motorbike, it will invariably happen when it is in motion, and the result could be fatal.

An emergency job on the road, which should not be used as an example, as it is wrong and dangerous. Always clamp work down properly when using a disc cutter.

Arc welding is the most useful type in the shed. The basic equipment is not too costly and, as experience grows, it becomes more helpful for complicated jobs. Stick welding (manual metal arc, or MMA) uses a rod of metal coated with a flux that provides the protective environment for the metal to fuse.

Prep

Clean all metal surfaces of rust, oil and paint, using a wire brush in the disc cutter. Put bevels on touching edges, where needed, to get good penetration of the weld. This is essential if the weld is to be polished out. Set up the pieces in position, using magnets to hold them or clamps positioned away from the weld. If you have to hold it in position, make sure your gloves are good and will not be burned by being too close.

For tacking together, use a maximum size of 2.5mm rod, or a smaller size for stainless steel. Do not use mild-steel rods on stainless, as the weld will rust; on the other hand, you can use stainless to tack mild steel. Store rods in a warm, dry place, such as an airing cupboard or in the plate warmer on cooking range, then warm them up in the oven before use, to make them work better.

Spot Weld

Make sure the rod is secure in the holder and the piece earthed with the crocodile clamp. Have a piece of earthed scrap to hand for practice, or start the rod. Set the amperage on the welder to the correct rod size – most will have this info on the dial, with the rod box giving the range for the size; use the middle setting to start. Holding the rod quite close to 45–60 degrees, gently touch the scrap with the rod end to start the arc, immediately lifting off fractionally to get it going. The aim is to produce a nice round pat of weld (not a run), which quickly joins the metal, with no overfill.

As the rod is moved away from the metal, it will flare and sputter; if it is too close, it will weld itself in and stick. If the rod sticks to the metal, release it from the holder and knock it off; resist the urge to grab it, as it will be hot! The retrieved rod may have lost flux from the end, so scratch it gently, arcing across the scrap, until it is level again.

Practise until you can just touch the edge of the pieces and, with a quick flare, produce a nice neat tack. If you hold for too long, it will burn through. If it is too quick, only one side will be melted or have weld on.

As the spot weld cools, it will contract and pull, so the piece may lift on the other side. Gently push it back down and then tack. Always tack at least two sides, to prevent it getting knocked off in transit to the professional welder.

My daughter, Blossom, practising her skills wearing a sensible apron and photo-reactive mask. This helmet is much easier to work with than the older masks.

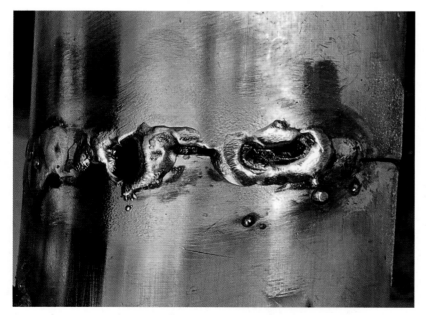

Beware of power settings that are too high, or large rods, as they can burn through thin metal on tubes and brackets, causing holes that need to be filled. This also happens if the gap is too big, as the voltage increases and will cause spatter.

Stitch Weld

Another way of making a join – say, for larger brackets – is to use a short run of welds, known as stitch welds. As before, get the rod at an angle of 45–60 degrees and get the spark. As it ignites, gently push the rod towards the weld while moving the point backwards; rotate the point of weld very slightly to build up metal. Do this in 15–25mm runs. Getting the knack for this will take a bit of time. If you go too slowly, metal will mount up, making undercut and trapped slag, or you will burn through the piece. If you go too fast, it will be underfilled and look stringy and messy – this is commonly known in certain circles as 'chicken-shit' welding.

TIG and MIG Welding

MIG welding uses a wire-fed gun, while TIG uses an electrode tip and a hand-fed rod. The equipment is more expensive to purchase than an arc kit and requires a whole new set of techniques. If there is a desire to start welding at this higher level, it is probably wise to undertake some dedicated training, or ask your friendly professional welder to let you have a go.

The same goes for brazing and flame welding – there is too much information for one book, but they are all

earth clamp

The earth clamps that come with budget welders tend to be pretty shoddy, eventually giving poor contact that will not help welding. Either buy a sparkly new heavy-duty one or hunt around a scrapyard or second-hand tool shop for a decent used item. They do not have insulation on the handles and can get hot, so be careful removing it after welding.

*TOP RIGHT: Samples of welds: (*bottom left*) two spot welds and a stitch; (*bottom right*) a full weld. The rest are examples of how not to do it, by arcing up, going too fast or using too much power. If you get some scrap and practise, you will find that basic welds are not that difficult.*
ABOVE RIGHT: TIG welds are the strongest. It is cost-effective to get them done at a fabrication shop rather than buying all the kit.
RIGHT: Mike, a friendly welding hero, finishing some lovely aluminium work.

LEFT: TIG weld undercut and overfilled. It is probably strong enough, but it is the wrong application to find out if it is not. One rule of thumb with welds is that a good weld should also look lovely.

BELOW: Aluminium bodywork tacked together.

techniques that are satisfying to learn and use.

Safety

Always wear the correct mask for welding. An auto-darkening one is best, as you do not have to flip it down and then find your weld point. The strong UV light of the arc will burn the cornea and causes arc eye; this happens very quickly and will give intense eye irritation for a long while afterwards. Never look at welding in progress and make sure that anyone in the shed is aware when you are working.

Do not look at a fresh weld without eye protection, as slag (the black crust) from a cooling weld can ping off and fly a good distance. This is very hot material and the tiniest bit in the eye will mean a trip to hospital.

Fumes from welding can be dangerous, although this should not be a problem with a few tacks here and there. Wind does not affect the weld, so if in doubt, take it outside.

The little hot blobs that shoot off during welding are called spatter. They will burn instantly and have a habit of dropping on hands, so wear long gloves. Short gloves will allow only a bit in but will also prevent quick access to it, making it worse than bare hands!

TOP: *Checking the seat fits after welding up the seams.*

ABOVE: *Partway through the sanding down and polishing for the BMW project.*

Shed welders can often be identified by the numerous burn holes in their t-shirts; get an apron in thick cotton or leather. The risk of fire from spatter landing and smouldering in a corner is high, especially in wooden sheds with oily rags, fuels, and so on. Keep a CO_2 or dry-powder fire extinguisher handy, and do not use water, as there is a danger of shock.

A lovely example of riveted bodywork gives a steampunk look to fabrication.

A cheap riveting kit and a better gun bought second-hand.

Getting an electric shock from a welder is painful. It is not fatal to a healthy person, but it should be prevented by ensuring that all cables and equipment are kept in good condition.

RIVETING

Thin sheet metal can be joined together using rivets. The most common method is pop-riveting (blind riveting), which is good for building boxes or interesting bodywork without the need to weld. It can also be a good detailing technique. Basically, a hole is drilled through two sheets, the rivet is inserted and then it is expanded on the inside to lock the rivet and metal together. Pop rivets were designed so they could be inserted and fixed without needing access to both sides of the metal; in the old days, solid rivets would be inserted and then beaten down on the inside to form a locking head.

Apart from a drill, the only kit needed for riveting is a rivet gun. As usual, the cost will increase as the quality improves, but it is worth buying a decent model, either new or second-hand, as very cheap ones are likely to let you down. The gripping collets are the parts that will wear out most often and can be purchased separately.

Size and Material

Rivets can be bought in bulk, which makes sense. To find out which size to use, go to the local trade fasteners shop and buy a variety of sizes and lengths to practise with and assess before ordering a larger quantity. They are available in aluminium, steel, stainless steel and copper; on bikes, use aluminium or stainless for the structural bits, while copper is great for decorative work.

Method

To join two sheets together, mark out and drill holes to fit the rivet body tightly, along the edge of the upper sheet only. Line up the sheets and mark one hole, either at an end or in the centre of the bottom sheet, then drill it and place a rivet through each one. Slide the riveter nozzle fully down the wire (mandrel) and, pushing the sheets together, operate the levers. If the mandrel does not snap off on this

ABOVE: Samples of rivets, which come in all sizes and with different flanges. The riveted metal has used three lengths: (left) too short, (centre) correct and (right) too long.

RIGHT: The edges of drilled holes can be cleaned up and rounded over using a rotary burr; these come in a variety of sizes and shapes and are usually bought as a set.

BELOW RIGHT: As an alternative to rivet detailing, Pepe has used brass fasteners with domed nuts on his steampunk Guzzi.

turn, release the levers and slide the nozzle back down to the rivet, then operate again. Now start on the rest of the holes. Drilling through the holes one at a time, then riveting, then moving on to the next one, prevents buckling from misaligned holes.

Air Riveting

This is a step up from pop rivets, using a compressed-air gun to hammer in the rivets. The hole is drilled, a dome-headed rivet is placed in and a solid lump of metal is held against it on the inside. The gun is then placed on the rivet head and activated; this delivers a sharp action that flattens the inside of the rivet and leaves a nice domed head showing. If serious amounts of stylish rivets are envisaged, then this is the kit to get. Just make sure you have a compressor that produces enough charge.

LEFT: Getting imaginative with copper: a simple plumbing set-up using a gas valve and fittings works for a petrol tap.

BELOW: Fancy detailing is possible using easily available materials.

PROJECT: MAKING TABS

Adding non-standard parts to a bike means there will need to be some way of attaching them. The easiest way is to weld a bit of metal with a hole in to the frame; a very simple task. Making a tab that looks good enough and does the job just requires a bit of care, as explained here.

The Metal

Tabs can be made from any spare flat metal, as long as it is not too rusty – the pockmarks will not buff out without thinning the metal. The thickness for most applications – seat, tank, and so on – should be no less than 3 mill, going up to 5 for heavier parts or for more strength.

Marking Up

Apply masking tape on to the cleaned surface, and with a square draw in the centre line. Get a largish washer to draw the curved end and either strike parallel lines to the base (where it will be welded) or slope from the edge of the curve to widen at the base; whatever works is fine.

Mark the centre of any holes and centre-pop them. If the spacing of the holes is crucial, centre-pop the first one and then use dividers set in the dent to mark the next one. This allows for error in placing the first one.

Drilling

Pilot drill the holes and then full drill, ever so slightly larger than the bolt to be used, so that paint is not removed when fixing, and to give a slight margin for misplacement. Measure the placement of the hole(s) and mark the edge adjustment if they have moved off centre. Using a fine disc blade, cut the sides (unless you are using bar of the right width) and then cut to length. Put a bolt and nut into the hole, with a washer that matches the curve, then mount securely in a vice and cut off the corners of the curved end.

Cleaning Up

Round the end with a sanding disc, using the washer edge as a guide, and blend into the sides smoothly. Remove the nut and bolt and sand off any burrs, giving a nice smooth radius to the edges and the hole, so that paint lies on without weak corners.

BODYWORK

Forming thin sheets of metal to make bodywork and tanks is a time-consuming task and can seem daunting to the newbie, but do not fret. Shaping and building up a piece may be tricky, but it is fun and the result can be surprising. Obviously, complicated creations might not be achievable right away, but for rawness and craft feel, even simple shapes can be undeniably lovely.

As a complete amateur of panel beating, I decided to make an aluminium tank seat unit for one project. This was partly because I wanted something more interesting than the plain and rather characterless ones found in the shops, and partly because the shop-bought ones only really fit a certain type of frame rail – not the one I had stuck on my bike.

It is impossible to use only shed skills and tools to make a seat hump from one single sheet. Using aluminium meant that this was not an issue, as it was easier to build up from small pieces. This method makes shaping simpler and, if a mistake is made, the whole assembly does not have to end up in the bin.

The form is marked out to show where the pieces will meet to be welded. Using a flexible ruler, bend it around the form and draw lines at the highest points of a curve. These need to be straight in plan. Place a piece of paper over and transfer these lines on to it; if it will not lie flat, do an approximation, with a bit of allowance. Scissor-cut this shape out and trace on to the sheet, then cut out using tin-snips; always deburr the edges.

Setting out.

Shaping around washer.

Ready to attach to the frame.

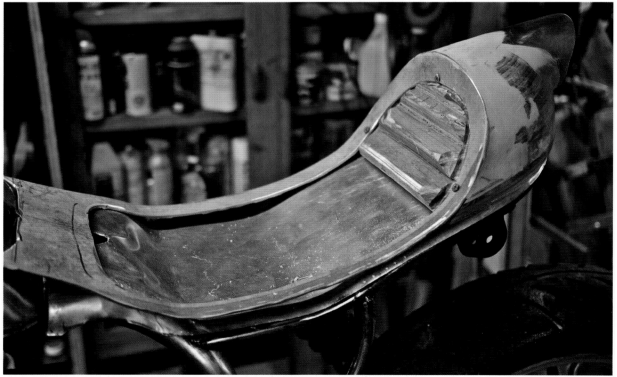

TOP: Sublime bodywork by Lamb Engineering. The things you can make using shed skills are limited only by how much you apply yourself, and your imagination.

ABOVE: If possible it is handy to have a shaped solid surface, known as a former, to work the sheet around. The rear hump was shaped to sit on the rear loop and give a curved seat bottom; this was accomplished by jigsawing oversize ply shapes, gluing them together, then working them to shape with the coarse flexi sanding disc. Holes were filled in with filler and then smoothed over. Other formers have included curved tubes, a fire extinguisher and a bowling ball.

Looking at the shape, figure which former is close to the curve. With it securely mounted, and starting from the centre, beat the metal consistently, radiating out as it starts to take on the curve. Use other spherical formers to get the curve going in two directions. This is a lot easier to do than explain, so it is best just to explore the shapes you can get and keep offering it up to the form. If it is curved too much, open it out a bit by hand. Once it is close to what you want, hold it tight in one place and dress it down using radiating small step taps until it is even closer. Keep it in place and mark where the join line is – by now, the shape may not fit in the original area – and then trim this seam with snips, or a fine disc that will not distort the metal again. Do this for all the sections, taping them together and trimming any overlap so that they are butt-jointed. The line along a curve needs to be straight; other joints can be played around with.

Take the form and the shapes to the welder. Where the shapes sit on the form exactly and butt up nicely, put a tack or two here, and then, with a combination of some mild dressing, pushing and holding in place (wear thick gloves, as it will get hot!), tack it all together. Work away from the first tacks, dressing as you go, ensuring the

skid marks

A rubber mallet may seem like a good idea, and indeed it is excellent for beating the aluminium sheet without leaving any hammer marks. What it does leave is an invisible smear of rubber (or derivative) on the surface of the metal. If this is not cleaned up before going to the welder, it will cause problems, as the contaminant will react with heat, causing craters and runs during welding.

TOP RIGHT: My bodywork kit, cobbled together from the shed, coped with producing the BMW seat unit.

ABOVE RIGHT: Sections of the shape are beaten round and tacked in place, then the next pieces are made. The shapes will need trimming as it goes together. Do not attempt a complete jigsaw from the start.

RIGHT: Dressing the seat base over the frame tubes is easy; just keep the overhang short, or it will buckle.

edges do not get kinked, then weld the joint, leaving plenty of meat to sand back and get seamless.

With increasingly fine discs and emery cloth, remove the lumpy parts of the weld until the surface is smooth, then polish as desired. If any holes appear, fill with weld and sand again.

TOP: *Following the frame up to the tank. Obviously, this work should be done before the frame is painted.*
LEFT: *Neat painted aluminium covers made by Keith on his Buell.*
BELOW: *The next stage will be working this tank blank to fit; watch this space…*

frame

Standard bike frames, designed to be built easily and cheaply by machines, with little thought for simplicity and elegance, have a multitude of brackets and mass-produced gubbins hanging off them. Obviously, if the bike is to have cleaner lines and different kit attached to it, then a cull of unwanted metal must take place. This is known as 'detabbing'.

Before the grinder is dragged out and the sparks begin to fly in the workshop a plan of attack must be drawn up. This is a task that can take some time and fiddling, but it is important to do it as, once your frame has been cleaned and painted, any further work or additions will be costly or require some ingenuity. The aim is to make the frame look as if it never had those brackets and that the new ones blend in smoothly with the whole.

The mock-up stage can be fun or frustrating, depending on how you choose to approach it, because it entails building the bike completely and, when everything is right, stripping it down again. Gather together all the components that need to be attached to the frame and get to it.

If you can, use original brackets to attach to, unless you think they are too ugly or too big or obtrusive, as this will help in lining up items such as the mudguards and so on.

ABOVE RIGHT: It is too easy to omit the steering stops when building a frame with new yokes, as it is not until the bike is moved around that they become useful. This is one solution that could have been neater if incorporated into the yokes; when mocking up, always have a checklist of items to be sorted out before painting.

RIGHT: A Beemer having a monoshock conversion. Nothing has been removed from the frame yet, and will not be until the mock-up has been finished, ensuring all fits together well. Always take time at this stage to sort out as much as possible before getting the disc cutter out.

ENGINE MOUNTS

The engine mounts need to stay in the same position, although they can be tidied up or replaced with neater options. If you are keeping the same ones, bolt up the engine tight and do alterations to the others as needed. If they are to be replaced, cut them off before the engine goes in, remembering to keep enough mounts to securely and accurately locate the lump; do it piecemeal if it helps. Clean up the scars before putting the engine back in securely, then attach and bolt up the new mounts securely in place on the engine. Shape these to butt up to the frame and, where they make contact, tack in place. If the welding is to be done by a professional, so that it looks really good, place the tack out of sight as much as possible. Make sure the welding proper will not pull them out of line by tacking on both sides. Ask the welder to do it as stitching from side to side rather than as a full weld on one side in one hit.

If you want to make some new engine mounts, secure the engine so that it is in the correct position and alignment, then measure the distances of the centres of two of the holes and mark them on a template. Take the distance of the third hole from the centre of the other two and, with a compass/dividers, scribe arcs of the distances from them; the third hole is at the point where they intersect. Drill the template to check it works and adjust if necessary.

Draw up the mounts full size, to your preferred design and dimensions.

Template offered up for fit.

The metal used is a reject sprocket of good-quality aluminium. The template is laid on to get the position of the rough shape, and then the centres are popped in and the edges scribed.

These can either be sent off for water-jet cutting or used for making up in the shed (*see* illustrations).

To strengthen holes through the frame, take measurements of width and drill out the holes, then slide a tube through the hole and weld in place. Drilling through a frame without strengthening the holes can create a weak point and possibly lead to failure.

Components will be attached either by a tab or into a threaded hole, so get some flat bar and knock up a collection of over-length tabs with the hole end neatly rounded off clean and ready to be painted. Cut to length as needed, to attach to the component and tack them in place. Remember to protect any component that could be marred

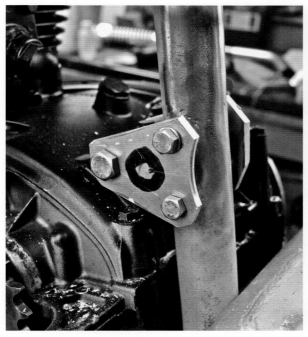

TOP RIGHT: *Two roughly cut-out plates are clamped together and drilled (pilot first, then full). Shaping and detail will take place later – once they fit, there is no rush until the bike is finally assembled.*

ABOVE LEFT: *Before detailing they are mounted and used to hold the engine while building.*

ABOVE RIGHT: *Waterjet-cut mounts being lined up to the frame.*

RIGHT: *Grip and drill: holding two pieces of aluminium together with mole grips for drilling, using a strip of sandpaper to prevent the jaws marking the metal.*

clearance

When mounting components, make sure there is clearance for attaching cables or doing up nuts, that no electrical contacts touch metal and it can be removed easily enough.

If the seat is yet to be knocked up, put a couple of tabs in sensible (symmetrical) locations, to marry up with the future base bolts. Put these level with the top of the frame tube, so that the heads of bolts or nuts will be out of sight.

TOP: New engine mounts being set up before the tabs are welded on to the frame. Everything must be true and level, checked using the height gauge; mount a vernier or sliding square in a drill vice to do this job.

ABOVE: Threaded insert nuts are neat, safe and secure as attaching points, drilled into the frame and welded in place. Stainless ones will not corrode internally when the paint is stripped off during assembly.

by weld spatter or excessive heat. It really is essential to have a small welder for this type of work, because just marking the spot where the tab fits, before taking it elsewhere to be welded, is fraught with problems if they are subsequently attached out of true, even by the slightest margin.

Other options for mounts are tubes that form small eyes, possibly threaded internally, welded to the frame – if welding a threaded piece, put a greased bolt in before tacking, to keep the inside clean and usable. Tubes are a bit awkward to tack in as the undercut of the tube stops good contact when using welding rods; so either flat a side to the frame or tack carefully. Do not weld on the end to which the component is being attached, or where a flat surface is needed for bolting against.

If a new attachment is to be fixed next to an old unwanted tab, cut this off and do the cleaning and finishing first, as it will be difficult working around the new tab. Unless you are a dab hand at this, do not attempt to reshape a tab in situ. Instead, cut a new tab to the shape required, all cleaned and finished, ready to be painted.

CUTTING BACK AND CLEANING OFF

Ready to go? Now strip the whole bike down, bag any engine bolts you need to be swapped for stainless, and get it outside ready for the work.

Set up the disc cutter with a fine metal blade – not the old-school 3mm thick ones – and set the frame securely in position. It might look cool doing this with the wheels in, but it limits the amount of moving around you can do, so a loose frame is the best bet. Gently score a line across the tab about 3 mill above its weld and gradually cut through the metal in strokes. Do not jam it in and try to go through in one pass, as it could catch, break the blade or jerk the cutter out of your hands.

Many brackets have a captive or welded nut on them to bolt into, like this shock mount. When making new, use stainless nuts, as they will not rust when the paint is taken off the thread. Note the plugs going to be welded into the ends of the cut tubes to neaten them up and prevent water ingress.

With the bulk removed, mount a solid grinding disc and, once again in calm passes, take the stub down into the weld, stopping about a couple of mill above the frame line. Do not attempt to use this for rounding down the last bit, as it is not gentle enough and will gouge the tube.

Now, using a decent sanding disc (about 60–80 grit – the type made of overlapping strips of abrasive cloth is

the best), start working down to the tube line. Take off the metal in strips along the weld and, as the tube is neared, take off the pressure and almost float the disc over the surface by rotating the disc around the tube. Always work along the tube. Do not go around at right-angles or you will end up with ridges and valleys. If it is done carefully, the surface finish of the exposed tube should be lightly and evenly scored,

Metal grinding disc.

Sanding or flap disc.

Abrasive kit for cleaning frames.

with no deep scratches – any deep cuts will need to be smoothed out and will show up as ripples in the paint, which will not look good.

For a final touch, a wire-brush attachment on the disc cutter can be used to blend in the rubbing down to a near-perfect finish.

It now needs to be finished smooth using abrasive paper or wet and dry. Alternatively, you can buy green and red flexible sponge diamond pads from a stonemasonry tool shop. They cost a bit, but never wear out and will pay for themselves very quickly. Rub down until all the other marks are gone and the tube is as smooth as possible, using clean water to stop clogging. This will take some time and elbow grease but it is essential if you are to achieve a nice clean line; any imperfections will show in the paint, and by then it will be too late to do anything about it.

While the tools are at hand, have a good look at the frame for any imperfections in the manufacturer's work, such as lumpy welds, that would benefit from blending in better with a nice TIG weld by someone who cares. Tiny metal beads can often be seen near welds. This is spatter and can be knocked off using a cold chisel and hammer. Do not gouge it off; strike it from the side, it will shear off, leaving no trace.

Plates or gussets are often only welded partially, leaving a gap where muck and rust can accumulate as the paint protection has failed to get around the inside. Clean the old paint off and get these welded up neatly.

FRAME CHECKLIST

Once you have done the cutting back and cleaning off, and depending on the order in which you plan to do things, you can put everything together again and start attaching the new mounts, get them welded up properly and send the frame off to be shotblasted and painted. However, before you do all that, have a final look at everything – this is where building it all raw helps – and work your way down the checklist.

- Headstock: is the steering lock being removed? Remember to fill in the hole when it has been cut off. Steering stops are needed to set the turning lock: are these welded on or does a tab need to be fixed for mounting? If wiring is to go through frame, drill, clean the holes and thread a guide wire through ready to pull the loom through.
- Tank and seat mounts: set them up so the tank sits correctly and the seat can be put on securely without having to dismantle a lot of other items.
- Are brackets needed for the coil mount, horn mount, battery box mounts, rear mudguard, footpegs or rearsets?
- Side-stand mount with provision for spring – does the stand need a stop to rest against?
- Check exhaust hangers and shock mounts.
- Tap any holes used for attaching clips, and so on.
- Clean off all spatters. Visually check tubes for grinding scars and clean up where necessary. Deburr any sharp edges and holes.

Then you can get it painted!

LEFT: *A factory weld and spatter, which is easy enough to remove.*

BELOW LEFT: *A simple jig for drilling holes in tubes: two pieces of centre-drilled bar, one pilot hole and one bolt size, are welded on to a section cut from a larger tube. This can be clamped on to the tube with mole grips.*

BELOW RIGHT: *Drilling a blind hole (one that does not come out the other side) can be made easy by wrapping tape around the bit at the depth required.*

Putting the engine into the frame is awkward and can end up scratching new paint. The simpler and safer way is to lay the engine on its side on some softening, manoeuvre the frame over and on to it, then slide engine bolts in.

Frame with new seat loop added, freshly painted and ready to build.

JOINING TUBES

As you become more confident with working on bike frames, you may decide to tackle the addition of extra tubing, whether as bracing or to join on to the end of an open tube, perhaps adding a rear loop. This is basic work that can be done with a disc cutter and arc welder, but, as the parts will probably be structurally integral to the frame, it is recommended that you tack them in place first and then get the joints welded up by someone competent using MIG or TIG, or even brazed.

Do not dive straight in and start on the frame; get a couple of bits of tube and have a practice first to get a feel for the process. Once this is mastered, there will be no problem doing it for real. There are sites online where it is possible to download a printable template that gives the shape of the cut to be made; all you need to do is fill in the dimensions and angles.

Attaching a New Tube

First, with a wire brush attachment on the grinder, clean all traces of paint and rust off the area to be worked on, down to a shiny surface, on both the frame tube (FT) and the new tube (NT).

Mark up on the frame where the top and bottom of the NT will be attached, and clamp the tube in position behind the FT. Draw a line on the NT along the centre of the tube on the side touching the FT, then a line that follows the FT on both ends.

Now pull the NT out and draw lines, parallel with these lines, one-third of the diameter of the NT away from the FT line.

Intersect these with the centre line, and from the intersection point take lines to touch the FT line at the top and bottom.

Cutting and Shaping

Secure the tube with the centre line uppermost and cut the tube vertically just on the edge of the sloping line. Make it as accurate as possible. It will be easier with a mechanical hack or chop saw, but the job can also be done carefully with a fine disc in the disc cutter; check all edges are level with their opposite number.

Offering it up will show that it is already a fairly good fit. A bit of shape grinding will make it better – an oldish segmented paper sanding disc on the cutter, with a nice curved profile, will help with this. Clean out the inside of the cut, giving the external angle cut a slight inward chamfer.

First markings.

tube

Hire a hydraulic tube bender for your work.

Common pipe used for building and other purposes is not designed to be bent in the same way as tube, so get your supplies from a reliable source.

All marked up.

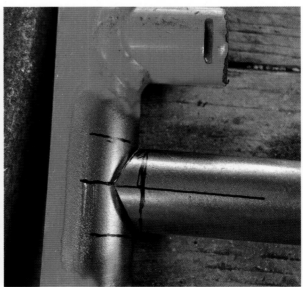

'Corners' cut off, it is starting to look close.

ABOVE: : Adding some curve with a flap wheel.

RIGHT: A simple but efficient method for a good result.

Trying the plug for fit.

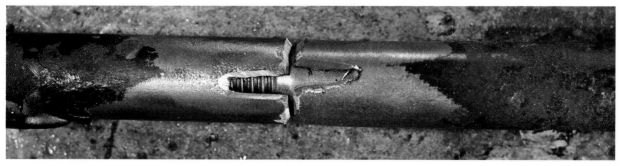

Grind slots to allow more weld and increase strength.

Grind and polish the welds back to the tube lines, filling any blemishes with a spot of weld and taking it down again.

Work the shape equally at both ends and keep offering it up for snugness; it may be necessary to work the long (internal) cut down a bit more to let it seat.

When it fits, a bevel edge can be put on the outside of the lip for weld penetration, then it can be secured in place with a tack weld ready for welding proper.

Two Tubes Together

When the back rails have been cut to take a new termination or loop, the tubes used should be of the same diameter and wall thickness as the original, with square-cut ends and cleaned of all burrs. With a standard metal cutting disc (not the fine one), cut a slot in all the ends to be joined, about 10–15mm long, running in line through the tube. Put a bevel in the slot to allow weld penetration and bevel the cut ends as well. Putting bevels in here allows the weld to be placed well in the metal body, so it can be polished out without losing strength.

A solid plug about 30–40mm long should be fashioned to fit snugly inside the tube; this can be turned from a bolt if necessary, as long as it is a snug fit. If your slug is too big, take it down on the lathe, or clamp it in the pillar-drill chuck and sand it down as it rotates. Do not just grind it, as it will end up misshapen and loose.

Tap the slug halfway into the FT; to prevent it slipping in too far, tack-weld it on the end of one of the slots. Drive the NT on to the slug until the tube ends meet and tack at the other side, then get it welded properly, making the weld proud of the surface.

STRENGTHENING

The simplest method is to mount a plate that starts at the junction and is welded to the intersecting tubes. This gives added rigidity to the design and can be quite neat. Make a template from card to run along the centre of the tubes – not on the outside or inside – and cut out the shape from metal plate. To give it some form rather than leaving it as a plain triangle, flow a curve into the unconnected side or drill some holes to lighten the effect. Rub down and smoothly radius all exposed edges, and rub down the

A joint of two tubes at an angle is potentially a weak spot in a frame, especially if there is unequal or one-sided loading in the set-up. To alleviate this, some strengthening or support should be incorporated in the form of a gusset or brace.

Where the new loop hits the frame, a gusset has been put on top of the shock mount to give support.

frame tubes where it will sit. Make sure all the surfaces have a suitable finish for painting. Having it in the centre of the tubes allows both sides to be welded, so locate it correctly, tack in place, then get it welded up.

Line up the new tube across its span, with some to spare.

If the tubes welded on to the frame are projecting and have to support a weight, such as a new rear-frame loop for the seat, then it will probably be necessary to put in another tube to act as a support.

Mark a line across it, following the existing tubes and then parallel to this draw another line one-third diameter distance at each end past the first line.

At right-angles to the line, draw through the centre of the first line to the second line. Where it intersects, draw sloping lines back to the first.

Cut along these lines and work into a smooth inner curve to butt up to the original tubes. This will have to be done in tandem to get it to seat correctly.

When it is a snug fit, bevel the edge slightly for weld penetration and tack into place for the final weld.

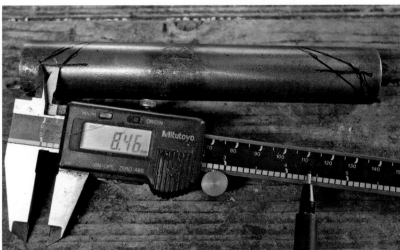

LEFT: *Marking up.*
BELOW LEFT: *First cut.*
BELOW RIGHT: *Try for size, working both ends incrementally together.*

painting

THE SPRAY AREA OR BOOTH

Getting a coat of paint on to metal is not difficult. It is doing it well that counts, so it is always worth practising on spare items rather than going straight to your own tinware. It is also important to have a decent place in which to spray. This can range from a screened-off area to a complete spray booth. Obviously, the amount of spraying to be done is the deciding factor. If a permanent spray booth is planned, buildings and insurance regulations must be observed. Assuming a one-off project, empty the area in which you will be working of precious items that will not benefit from a layer of paint, and set up sheets (tarpaulin, dust sheets or poly sheeting) to create a draught-free space with room to walk around the object.

As the materials are flammable and/or explosive, a large build-up is quite dangerous and an air-extraction system should be incorporated to keep a flow that prevents a build-up in the air. This will also, for larger projects done with spraying equipment, pull atmospheric paint away from the sprayer and the sprayed. The vent should have filters to trap the spray particles before they get to the fan. It is also advisable to wear a solvent mask; hang some masks outside the booth and change

Adding character to elements of a bike can be as simple as painting on some pinstriping. Practise the technique in the shed on old tanks or tinware – a tin of paint and a special brush are all you need.

For smaller items, set up a rack or a way to hang them so paint can be applied on all sides.

the filters regularly. Be aware that sporting a beard will seriously compromise the performance of a mask.

The booth should be warm, no less than 22 degrees centigrade, and cold metal should be allowed to warm up before you start spraying. No naked flames!

Good lighting is essential for making sure nothing is missed or amiss and fluorescent tubes or portable site lamps are good for this. Do not rely on an old one with powerful halogen bulbs, as these get very hot and react badly to liquid.

Set up a stable stand on which to mount larger pieces and fit fixed rails for hanging smaller items. If it is all organized properly, you should be able to walk in with the prepared item and secure it in place for spraying without having to put it down and possibly ruin its finish.

Once the spraying area or permanent booth has been set up, it is time to spray, but not before the real work has been done in terms of preparation.

PREPARATION

It may seem obvious that the easiest thing to make a difference to a bike would be changing the colour or adding decoration. Why not just drop it off at the powder-coat shop and collect it later? The problem is that this will get you just one colour and it will not have the depth and character that an individual paint job can provide.

Painting tanks and mudguards yourself is not that difficult, but it is time-consuming, mainly because the real trick to doing a good job is preparation.

Chemical Cleaning

If you are planning to paint on top of existing paintwork, check what is compatible with the original. Use a rag soaked with thinners to wipe the

Smaller parts that are spray-painted can be baked in the oven to toughen up the finish.

For that lived-in look, just let nature take its course, with a bit of wear here and some corrosion there. To preserve just the right amount of decay, dust off and wax on, or, for a more permanent effect, use clear gloss or matt lacquer.

surface. If the colour comes off, then it is an air-dry paint; if not, it must be powder-coated or urethane. Make sure you use the correct paint.

For a complete paint job, from the ground up, all the original paint and rust must be cleaned off. Take all the parts to be painted off the bike, put the smaller pieces into Ziploc bags and stack neatly; now is the time to get new rubber grommets, and change out the fasteners for stainless. Label all the fasteners and other bits, and put them in a safe place.

Stripping with a liquid paint stripper is messy and smelly, so you will need good ventilation or a mask. As long as you have due regard to the hazards, it is easy to do at home. The problem with modern strippers is that they are less powerful than before, due to health and safety standards, so the work may need to be done in layers. Lay out newspaper to work on, or do the stripping in a trug or bowl, to contain all the mess.

Wear glasses and coveralls, as the liquid will burn and irritate, and have some water and a sponge nearby to wash off any splashes. Use the water to neutralize the stripped surface afterwards, too. Wearing decent protective gloves that will not dissolve with the stripper, pour an amount into a glass jar. Always put the lid back on the tin to prevent the solvent evaporating, which will quickly render it ineffective. Use a cheap paintbrush to blob the stripper on to the paint and gently smooth across. Do not thin it out too much, just cover about a square foot at a time, then let it go to work. When the reaction of bubbling and peeling has stopped, use a plastic scraper to remove the sludge from the metal and drop it into a waste container. Do not use anything that will scratch the piece, as the marks will need polishing out. Repeat as necessary until all the paint has been removed, it may need scrubbing out of corners with a stiff-bristled brush.

Using Fire

Paint can be removed effectively from small items – not fuel tanks – by putting into a fire, and scrubbing with wire wool and polishing. This has also been used for frames and bigger pieces, but it is not the best way and the amount

A thin layer of paint will come off using paint stripper almost as fast as it can be brushed on. Once dissolved, the residue can be scraped off and rinsed clean.

friends in good places

Anyone working on bikes should make friends with their local industrial powder-coating company, to the point at which it is possible to drop in and get something blasted clean while you wait. The lunch break is a good time to visit and a spot of cash or a four-pack will make sure you are always welcome. It could save you having to collect all the bits together to go in the system, with the waiting that that entails. If you develop a good relationship with the right people, you might be able to drop small items, such as stands and covers, in to be blasted and powder-coated while you go off and run some other errands, and then pick them up a couple of hours later.

There is a wealth of services and skills available, often in one-man shows, on industrial estates up and down the country. They are indispensable for custom work, so be friendly and respectful and take care to build up a good network. And always pay promptly.

Vapour-blasted fuel tank; this is the most efficient method for stripping tinware back to metal.

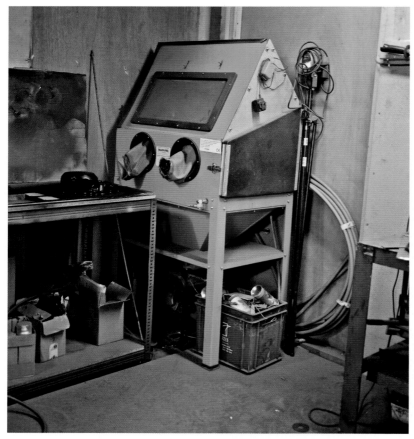

A blast cabinet will make short work of stripping smaller items. Check out the prices second-hand.

body filler

Body filler should always be applied to bare metal, otherwise it will come adrift in time. Mix up well and apply immediately to a clean dry surface. Do not attempt to shape right away, just get it on and smooth it in. It is easier and more controllable to fill by layers. Once a layer has set, sand it down with coarse grit and plenty of water to remove dust. Dry thoroughly, blow clean with airline and wipe with solvent cloth before the next layer. When you are getting near to the finish line, start using finer paper and blend in seamlessly to the metal. Any pits should be washed, blown clean and then filled as you go.

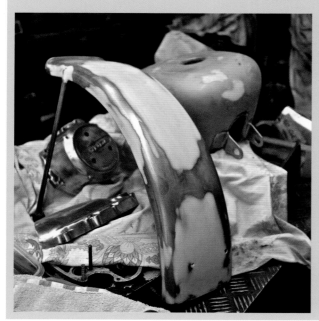

Using a large amount of filler to renovate an old mudguard

of work needed to clean them down is hard to justify when they can be stripped or abrasive-blasted.

Blasting

Abrasive particles fired at the paint is the most efficient way of removing surface finishes, rust and other accretions from metal, with an end result that will be scrupulously clean and ready to work on. Different levels of intensity are obtainable, depending on the material used. Shot- and sand-blasting are the most aggressive and will leave a rougher surface, while bead-blasting is gentler and vapour-blasting, the softest, can give almost a polish to metal. The result can be dependent on the skills of the blaster, but it will always be quick and relatively economic compared with the time taken cleaning down by hand. This, combined with the uniformity of finish, means that it really is the best option.

For cleaning smaller pieces, there are cheap sand-blasting kits that attach to a compressor and work with dry sand from DIY stores. The next stage is to buy a blasting cabinet; although the outlay can be a bit hefty (it is not worth buying the cheapest option), it may well pay for itself as you can cut out travel and time waiting for work to be done, as well as cleaning lots more stuff that could benefit from some attention – rusty tools, household kit, and so on.

THE PAINTING PROCESS

Once you have cleaned up your items, it is time to start painting.

Using a lint-free cloth, spray a bit of thinners or acetone on to the tank and wipe down scrupulously. If any oil or other residue remains, it will ruin the finish. Mask over all holes, to prevent paint getting inside, as fuel will wash it off and into the carbs.

Masking Up

Designs that can be put on to tinware are restricted only by your imagination and skill, so if you have a particular wish, it is worth trying out some practice pieces. When masking up, use special low-tack automotive tape that will not leave adhesive on the surface or stick too well. Lay the tape on and, if possible, form curves with the same

Masking up with paper to shield the non-painted areas.

piece as the straights to avoid dogleg transitions. It is possible to trim tape in situ using a new scalpel blade, either free hand or following a template, but be careful not to score the paint.

For a fiddly design, it may be effective to cut the masking to shape before applying, to reduce the risk of a slip or mistake on the fresh paint. Get a flat pane of glass or mirror, give it a really good clean, and polish dry using newspaper. Lay the tape out on this, with enough spare to cut out the design. Be logical in the placing of strips so that the design is not composed of loads of fiddly little scraps, and also be aware that going from flat glass to curved metal may cause some distortion. The trick to getting it right is experimentation. Cut out the design using a fresh scalpel blade; blades should be

renewed often, as they will soon blunt and tear the edge of the tape.

When you have completed the design, peel the tape off the mirror from the outer edge and locate a point at which to start laying it on to the tank. Wearing disposable gloves, carefully press down the tape along the cut, working away from the first adherence point; it may be necessary to lift up and redo bits, but with patience all will come good. Fancy designs of varying density may require sections of tape to be removed during the spraying. Have these laid on top and fold over a tab to allow them to be gripped easily and pulled off later.

Once the tape is on, affix clean newspaper to the back of the design tape, masking off the rest of the tank and parts not to be painted. When spraying,

do not spray against the edge of the tape as it will cause a ridge; always direct the nozzle straight down to get the best results.

Using a Rattle Can

Investing in good spraying equipment will be quite costly, and can really only be worth it for those doing a lot of work. As this exercise is assumed to be a one-off job on a tank or other part of a bike, the easiest route is to use spray cans. These are widely available in a huge range of colours and no specialized equipment is needed to get a good finish.

Set up the piece to be painted securely, in whatever position it is to be painted from; do not get clever and mount it so that it can rotate – you move, not the item. Warm the paint up by standing the can in a pot of hot water for ten minutes, then dry it off so no drops of water can spoil the paint, and shake for two minutes to mix.

Spray a burst of paint on to something waste to clear any droplets that may have formed, then, starting past the item, spray lightly as you move the can parallel with the surface in horizontal lines. Move smoothly and quickly, to prevent too much build-up, which could run. Use even strokes to cover the surface in a light film. Stop for a couple of minutes and then repeat, building up an even layer of paint; change the angle of attack if necessary, to get into seams and recesses.

After each coat, invert the can and spray to clear the nozzle, then, before

First coats of colour, done using a modern paint that acts as both primer and topcoat.

LEFT: With the colour done, stick on the pinstripe tape. The older auto-parts shops can be a treasure trove of interesting and useful stuff, with a wide range of paints and other decorating items.

BELOW: Flatting down prior to the application of lacquer. Every time you go to a finer grit, rinse off all the mess and empty the water container out; this prevents scratching by any fragments from previous rubbing.

the next coat, spray test on a waste piece to ensure there are no clogs or drops waiting to be put on to the tank. If any blemishes appear in the coat, there must be some contamination from an incompatible material, so rub out back to metal and clean again. Ensure that the edges of the rubbed area are feathered smoothly, to prevent contours building up.

Faded-in edges, where the colour gets weaker away from the edge, can add character, but do not look as as natural as the good ones look. On a waste test panel, spray along the tape, keeping the centre of the spray build-up in the same position relative to the edge at all times, and the speed of traverse constant. After a bit of practice at this, the fun aspect will kick in and you can begin to vary the effects as you wish.

Masking up discs for painting. The curves are overlaid and then cut with a scalpel; blades are binned after trimming each disc, to prevent a rough edge.

Primer and Base Coat

Metal is not the best surface for paint to stick to, so a couple of layers of good primer should be applied and allowed to dry. Rub down with 800-grit and use lots of clean water to take out any imperfections, rinse off the tank and allow it to dry. Before applying the base coat, wipe over with a thinner-dampened cloth to remove any dust.

The base coat can be the final colour before lacquering over, or it can be used to build up a design or panels.

Be very diligent in applying it, building up thickness over the session by many thin coats. To get a really smooth finish, rub down using 800- to 1200-grit, be critical and inspect it closely for scratches and imperfections. When you are happy with the quality of the surface, either apply topcoat and lacquer, or mask up for design.

Get all the imperfections rubbed down before the final coat of paint, or lacquer. Lacquer goes on thicker from a rattle can and it takes longer to cure, so do not build up the layers too fast.

Once the paint is well cured, apply a good-quality wax polish to protect it and make it easier to clean.

After the paint has dried down, brackets and small bits of the bike can be put into the oven at 180 degrees centigrade for at least half an hour, to 'bake' the paint. This will make it much tougher.

Troubleshooting

The following is a quick checklist describing the more common paint problems, and indicating what to do about them. They will affect most beginners at some time and this really underlines the need for good preparation. Using materials that are influenced by the condition of the surface, environment and mixes can result in a lot of wasted time and effort. Always read the instructions on the tin!

- Small craters: caused by contamination from oil or grease. Clean thoroughly using the right solvent cleaner, then paint.
- Wrinkling: occurs when solvent pulls into old paint or recoating too late when spraying. Rub down and follow manufacturer's specs.
- Dull or hazy results: caused by insufficient ventilation or using cheap solvents. Cut back and respray.
- Bleeding: the result of solvent dissolving older paint. Use a sealer first, then paint.
- Cracking: caused by too much build-up or accelerated drying. Remove and redo.
- Sags or runs: caused by spraying too close or too slowly. Wipe off with solvent immediately or leave and sand off.
- Orange-peel look: the result of too little thinner or heavy build-up on cool metal. Rub back and respray.
- Feather edging: solvent leaching into repaired areas. Use a good sealer/primer first.
- Scratches: the result of poor sanding of the surface. Sand and respray.
- Paint wiping off a tank: caused by using incorrect paint or lacquer. Use petrol-resistant product.
- Pinholes: caused by air bubbles in the filler. Rub back and seal.
- Blisters: caused by too much moisture in the air when spraying. Redo.

Because the spraying was done in a colder environment, the finished result was slightly textured. However, because the condition was even across the whole piece, it was decided to keep it and lacquer over it. When painting tinware at home it can be pragmatic not to get too precious if the bike is going to be used; the paint will cope. However, redoing it is another chance to build up skills and experience.

ABOVE: Sprayed discs.

BELOW: Finished and mounted with stainless bolts. The fork legs had the brackets removed, then were polished and powder-coated.

PROJECT: GEAR AND BRAKE LEVER

The alloy used in competition sprockets is good quality and once the teeth have worn they are just plates of metal. Here, using the nice curve available, a simple and effective lever is made up for gear or brake pedal, or both.

TOP LEFT: To make a pair, drill out the holes and clamp them together before grinding to shape.

LEFT: The finished lever has had a small section of alloy tube welded on the pivot point to house a bush and reduce lateral play.

BELOW: Gear lever made using an old spanner with welded on pivot and peg lugs; very steampunk.

PROJECT: BOBBER

Bobber Style

Back in the 1930s, buying a large-displacement bike in North America got you a lumbering dreadnought hauling weight in deep valanced mudguards (or 'fenders'), over-the-top exhaust plumbing and other running gear that would not look out of place on a farm vehicle. Meanwhile, factories and racers were knocking out stripped-down machines for track and board racing based on the standard production bikes, with lots of go-faster tweaks and improved handling. Understandably, this slick racing style would soon be adopted by youngsters and savvy mechanics looking for better performance from cooler steeds, and this is how the 'bobber' was born.

The true bobber is not a modified bike in terms of adding fancy parts. It is more a statement of biking intent, with all the garbage of racks, silencers and engine cowling thrown away, and the essential stuff, such as fenders, sets and lights, cut down to the minimum, or 'bobbed'. Now, technically, this would mean that any bike that had been made lighter and cleaner could be called a bobber, but in reality, when the term is applied to a bike, it refers to a very specific style. The word 'design' doesn't really apply to bobbers until after the war, when money and time became available to start customizing bikes and cars (hot-rods), making them pretty and raising their appeal to the less tearaway members of society; bobbers were unkempt, short and sharp.

The original bobber would be a big V-twin, in a rigid frame, with springers or girders up front, shortened fenders, a single seat and perhaps a smaller fuel tank. The bars were wide, the pipes were loud and riding was fun.

ABOVE: *My take on the bobber: a modified plunger frame holding a modern Sportster engine, supported on chunky spoked wheels with telescopic forks and plunger rear. Raw metal was the finish, with satin black detailing.*
RIGHT: *A sturdy XS650 engine sits well as a bobber powerplant; USD forks and second-hand Harley solid wheels add chunkiness.*

Inevitably the look has become mainstream and diluted to the point where it is now possible to buy a production 'bobber' straight from the factory; not just an oxymoron but a caricature almost equal to Jonny Rotten selling butter on TV.

Finding a Base for a Bobber

You may not always have the option to choose a bike to turn into a bobber. More often, it will be a case of running with what you already have, and the big decision will be how far to take it. Will the result be your considered interpretation or a mass of bolt-on bits? As with all custom bikes that are going to be ridden regularly, cleanliness and (implied) simplicity should be the aim.

Forget water-cooled bikes, unless you are confident that all the extra plumbing and radiators can be incorporated into the design. The best bobbers are air-cooled, but anything is acceptable if the owner is happy.

Bobbers sit low and horizontal to the ground, on a short wheelbase, with the main line running at a slope from the top yoke down to the rear spindle. Unraked standard-length forks create the last side of the triangle. These lines are brought about by the bike being a hardtail – a feature that is essential for the traditional look.

TOP: *A lightweight bobber based on the classic Triumph twin is slender and subtle with lovely paint. Drum brakes and a Bates light all add to the attraction.*
ABOVE: *This 45 has a patina that shows its age beautifully. The springers and jockey-shift make it as original as they come.*

The Finish

Originally, bobbers were made from used street bikes and tended to be quite roughly finished, with a beaten-up tank, worn leather seat and plenty of surface tarnish (known as patination nowadays). Bobbers were working bikes, popular before the advent of all the fancy colours and chrome of the 1960s, which led to the chopper culture. This means that, with a bit of imagination, a bobber can be made on the cheap, as new performance parts and high-tech materials are a long way away from the roots. Use well-worn parts for tanks, mudguards and seat, and search autojumbles and scrapyards for interesting lights and other parts that fit in with the scheme. Steampunk style, with lots of raw metal, rivets and rubbed-out paintwork, lends itself well to a solid utilitarian bobber.

The Frame

In terms of the frame, there are a couple of routes to go down. The simplest is to buy a ready-made rigid frame set up for your engine. While there is of course a cost to this, it can turn out to be economical, as it will significantly reduce the amount of work required. It also means that the frame will be a 'complete' design, rather than a standard frame with a welded-on tail, which can appear incongruous; it takes some skill to merge the two successfully.

The other option is to go for a second-hand frame. There have been a large number of frames made for Harley twins, Jap fours and old Triumphs, and when people change styles they can come up for sale second-hand. The advantage of these is that they can provide a lot of room to fit other engines, and ancillaries can be slotted in. Setting up an engine in a frame requires a decent workbench on which to build a jig, access to a welder and other machine tools, and some metalworking skills.

Setting Up

To set up the frame for engine mounting, you will need a dead flat work surface, preferably metal, although thick plywood will allow blocks to be screwed in. Before attaching or fixing anything in place, get it all level; put the rear spindle

Although modern Triumphs do not normally make great bobbers, this one works well.

Building a frame from scratch requires a jig, some good tool skills and an eye for a good line; Puptruck has got all that, and this will be a nice-looking bike

Second-hand frame built for big Harleys: once the post in the centre has gone, the engine will fit in, providing a good frame for little money.

145

centre distances

Knowing the exact distance of hole centres is crucial to making many parts on a bike; the dimensions of yokes, engine plates and brackets all need to be spot on at the design stage. Use a vernier held against the outer edges to get a distance, then halve the sum of the two diameters and subtract from the first dimension.

LEFT: Getting everything to line up: the plate clamped on the engine is flat against the sprocket and a bar can be laid against it and the rear to align them.
BELOW LEFT: A smooth Knucklehead sitting in a version of the 'softtail' frame; this gives rigid looks with proper suspension. The large frame brackets for this blend in well.
BOTTOM LEFT: Chunky Beezer with painted rims and split tank; it takes work to look this natural.

in through a hub with the sprocket on (it does not have to be the right one, as long as it fits the spindle; it will still allow the sprockets to line up). Then lift it to a height that lets the frame loops sit level off the deck. Tack supports on, so that it is locked in place.

Place the engine inside the frame and block it up until it sits in the correct place. Place a long bar through the mounting holes, projecting out either side; accurately measuring from the deck to this will allow you to wedge or manoeuvre the engine until each side is exactly the same height. Now measure the distance from this bar to the rear spindle. When the corresponding points are equal, then the engine is true and level in the frame. Clamp a dead straight bar across the face of both sockets – a builder's level is good for this – and make sure the engine is centred in the frame.

Now measure up for the first temporary mounting plates that will locate the engine; knock these up from some flat plate or bar and use washers to space. Do this for two motor mounts, carrying out any fine adjustment before tightening up, so that the engine is now locked in position. Make up decent tabs for the other mounts if necessary, or make templates for plates, bolt them to the engine and tack in place. Ensure they are securely fixed and that welding will not pull them out of position. Once these are done, remove the temporary mounts and make them properly.

Adding a Hardtail

There are various kits available to add a hardtail to a standard frame. These can come either as a pile of tubes and axle plates that will need setting up in a decent jig to get correct, or as a made-up hardtail ready to butt against the frame and weld in place. This level of frame work is within the remit of the competent shed builder, but as this is major frame alteration it is vital that it is done and fixed absolutely perfectly. Bad work here could cost a life.

With the aftermarket hardtail, check out the lines it gives from headstock to axle. The nicest bikes flow down smoothly, whereas some prefer a drop step at the seat mounting – a style that is taken to extremes in some custom bikes.

Wheels

Classic style is to have fat front and rear, based on the standard 16-inch rim and 5-inch tyres, but later you would see a skinnier tyre at the front, with the rims painted or in chromed steel with a deep centre ridge. Obviously this is down to personal choice, to suit you and the bike, but bobbers tend not to be extreme bikes. The best appear positively understated in their simplicity.

Buying made-up (second-hand) wheels is the best plan, even if they do seem pricey; the accumulated cost of buying in rim, spokes, hub and possibly bearings, plus the wheel-building charges and delivery, can be substantial. Hubs and rims need to have the same number of spokes, either 36 or 40. For safety's sake, the angles of the holes should match to each other – good wheel builders can sometimes get around this.

TOP RIGHT: *Sizing wheel spacers.*

RIGHT: *Big-diameter forks from a CCM enduro were shortened internally and fitted into modified second-hand slab yokes. The hand-guards did not make the final version, but have potential.*

wheel spacers

With a new wheel comes the issue of locking it into the correct place, which will entail new spacers. These will need to be exact and will involve some turning on the lathe. Slide two long spacers of tube (at least one of which should fit) into the hub, over the spindle on one side, to rest against the bearing race, and put the wheel in position. Slide the spacers apart so that one is against the bearing and the other against the axle plate, and measure the gap between them with a vernier. Add this to the combined length of the spacers to get the length of the wheel spacer. Turn the spacer from good-quality aluminium or steel; it should be a close fit on the spindle and seat securely against the bearing and the axle plate. Repeat the exercise for the other side, and then tighten up the ensemble to make sure everything turns and runs true. The technique is the same for the front-wheel spacers.

Steampunk loveliness, oozing retro charm; a lot of work has gone into this, and it shows.

Front End

When mocking up the bike it should sit level and work without having to stretch the forks, although an aftermarket frame may have the headstock pulled out more with a slight rake, so that a couple of inches extra may be needed. Old-school springers, similar to the originals, are back on the market now, available in varying levels of quality. If you are going to buy some springers, check out what is on other bikes and when you see a pair that suits, get the supplier's details. Using springers will also require new brake-mounting plates and fittings on the wheel, so that cost must be factored in.

Telescopic forks look good and have the advantage that they can be from the original bike, or can be tracked down second-hand. Clean them of reflectors, casting marks and extra brackets. Modern USD forks do not get used often with bobber lines, as they tend to look a bit clunky for a lightweight bike in a rigid frame.

Tank and Seat

Split tanks, like the ones on Harleys, are good, as are old-style British versions. The profile should taper or curve nicely down the front point of the seat. Do not be afraid of using a tank that leaves the spine of the frame exposed with well-thought-out mounts either made to be on display or tucked out of sight.

In terms of the seat, a solo sprung saddle is the original style and one that works only with hardtail-style bikes, so make the most of this. They are easy to make and cover, so go for materials that fit the bike, such as quality leather. You could even cut up an old jacket and use that. There are also plenty of aftermarket seats available, ranging from cheap Chinese to antique Bates. It is the fitting of them that can take some work, so mount up at the pre-paint stage. As they are meant to be sprung (which is essential for riding a hardtail), it may take a couple of attempts to get it right. The springs must support the rider's weight and bounce without grounding out. Make sure they do bounce – there are mini shock absorbers advertised for this, but, as they are spring-rated at a thousand pounds, they can be a literal pain in the butt.

Stance and Noise

Bars on a bobber can be whatever you want, from huge apes to mini club-mans. Most will look great, but what really counts is how comfortable and

A flea-market find – almost worth building a bike just to support it.

ABOVE: Lily checks out the riding position: ergonomics are often ignored in show bikes or extreme customs, but, as there is nothing worse than being unable to stand up after a long ride, some style compromise may be needed, or a decent alternative created.

RIGHT: Chris's wrapped pipes are not everyone's cup of tea, but the sound of shorty drag-pipes is my idea of music.

LEFT: *Oil tank: an aluminium fire extinguisher has good proportions for using as the body of an oil tank. The paint is removed and it is cut on a cross-cut saw with a metal disc to angle the filler cap.*

ABOVE: *The thickness of the walls allows threaded lugs to be welded on and, as a good conductor of heat, helps in cooling. If required, it would be possible to get slots turned in to make cooling fins. The fittings here are standard brass plumbing connections and copper tube, which are not too pricey and easy to work with.*

controllable the bike will be. Being doubled over or hanging off apes may look badass, but the strain on the legs and arms soon becomes telling on anything other than smooth tarmac or short journeys. If you want enjoy a bike properly, it must be tailored to the use it is going to get.

In terms of noise, bobbers should be loud and antisocial, so the pipes will need to be edging the legal limits; the paltry putter of the factory 'bobber', although described as a roar, rarely cuts the mustard, which is why there is a plethora of aftermarket exhausts available. In defence of rorty exhausts, remember the old adage, 'Loud pipes save lives', as people and hopefully dozing car drivers will certainly hear you coming.

Paintwork

Paint is a personal choice, as always, although a well-put-together bobber sporting skilful patination as a finish is always good. Old-school candy and metalflake work well. On a bobber, the tank and possibly the rear mudguard are often the only places to paint, so it is worth investing in a good design.

LEFT: *Using an existing lever or setting out to fit your design, centre-pop the centres for pivot and lever peg. Scribe or mark the outer design onto the plate and using a fine disc, cut out as close to the edge as possible.*

ABOVE: *Drill the holes and fix a large washer in place to use as a template to get a smooth shape, then work to with abrasive flappy disc.*

exhausts

One of the most common component swaps on a bike relates to the exhausts, or pipes. These changes have a lot to do with making the bike sound better and look different, but there can be practical reasons as well. The punishment that pipes endure on a bike means that the relatively thin metal of the system will not last as long as the rest of the bike. The likelihood of finding the original exhaust on an older bike is very small. On newer bikes, the limits set by emissions and finely coordinated working parameters tend to result in an excess of weight and a muted effect – and, once the lights are turned up for a closer look, it is notable how ugly many of them are. To keep production costs down, many pipes are just uncoated steel hidden behind shiny covers, creating gunge traps and allowing all the rot to carry on out of sight. It is understandable, then, that the average builder will want to upgrade.

For many bikes, especially the classic favourites and newer retro machines, there are aftermarket pipes aplenty. These range from reproductions of the originals to state-of-the-art computer-modelled performance systems. If you include custom versions and bespoke systems, the choice is huge.

ABOVE: A brutal take on an exhaust system for a four-cylinder bike – a bit anti-social but simple and effective.

The Law

It must be mentioned that there are legal requirements relating to the noise and emissions of motor vehicles; unsurprisingly, these cover bikes as well, so any of the advice given here must be taken with this in mind. The most recent restrictions apply clearly to modern machinery, but the regulations get a bit vague for examples over a certain age, so there may be scope for some creative leeway. If in doubt, talk to garage owners, check online

RIGHT: Two-strokes need a different type of exhaust from four-strokes, due to the nature of how the engine works performance relies a lot on the design; get it wrong and it may cost.

and, most helpfully, join a forum for your particular make and ask other members. Never be afraid to ask questions – most bikers love to chat about their bikes and how ingenious they are when it comes to building radical machines that push the limits, while remaining within the law.

WRAPPING

Many builders seem to be wrapping their exhausts, but it is a practice that, like many custom changes, has no practical or performance-related use. It is simply a trend that has caught on. The headers and manifolds of racing cars

and some bikes used to be wrapped, to prevent the heat from the pipe building up in the enclosed engine bays, but the cost of replacing the headers after each race became prohibitive; nowadays, if you look for wrapped pipes on a performance bike, you will be disappointed. Wrapping is useful for hiding

ABOVE: *Not every custom bike has to be top-notch; here a loosely wrapped exhaust adds the usual rustic look to the ubiquitous 'brat bike'. Unfortunately, the cheap plastic switches, painted-over fasteners and grubby carbs indicate that quality of build may have been sacrificed for show.*

LEFT: *Recycling at its best: an old car manifold adds a little steampunk style to a Knucklehead exhaust.*

headers that you do not want to be seen, but if they are in such poor condition, the last thing they need is a wet bandage. Bluing of stainless and chrome headers can also be hidden by wrap, but, if the pipe can rust – if, for example, the chrome has gone or it has been painted – then the wrap will trap moisture next to the metal. Heat and cold nights will also create the perfect environment for rust.

If you do decide to apply exhaust wrap, the job is simplicity itself. You will need a bucket of water, gloves, wrap and stainless cable ties, and a friend. Loosely wrap the exhaust, to get an idea how much bandage to cut off, then put it in the water to soften the strands. With your aide holding the pipe, wrap one turn at the inlet end and make very secure with ties. Keeping the bandage stretched to its limit, carefully roll it around the pipe with 5–10mm overlap until the end is reached. Fold the cut end under itself and secure well with ties.

CHOOSING PIPES: SHOP-BOUGHT OR HOMEMADE?

Look around and see what suits your build. There are numerous types, but stainless pipes over chrome are particularly recommended, as they will not corrode. The downside is that they discolour quickly compared with chrome (single tube pipes will always have this issue). Modern ceramic coatings are lovely to look at and the added cost can be worth it, although they are slightly more brittle and, once chipped, will rot. My personal experience with a custom set of ceramic pipes was not a positive one: apart from the fact they did not actually fit the bike they were made for, they also came with a warning that they should not come into contact with oil or petrol – a physical impossibility in a shed!

Get the new exhaust system before the frame is painted, and possibly before detabbing, as it might use original mounts. Mount it with the engine in and support it using blocks and cable ties to get it in the best position; pipes can flex so do not let it just hang from the exhaust ports while sizing up.

Engine vibration is transmitted to the thin metal pipes so they must not be held too rigidly close to the engine. The position of the mounting tabs should

Rare Triumph with lovely sectional exhaust curling around the engine.

Evo pipes were made in one piece to a template provided. When ordering bespoke pipes, get them in the schedule as early as possible, as some manufacturers (especially the good ones) are usually heavily booked up.

Bending the tube so that good curves are formed, follow the desired lines so it exits where the silencer is going. Use plenty of cable ties and gaffer tape to adjust and secure it so all is locked in place, remembering to pack out and allow clearance on the frame and engine.

Using whatever wedging is needed, lock the end into the exhaust port, fastening the clamp in place as well.

When the pipe is done it will need a flange to the inlet end for the clamp to hold it in place. This should be slid on before any fixing bolts are welded further down.

be no wasted effort; the only cost will be materials and time, so it is worth considering this as an option for your needs.

To create a mock-up, get hold of some ribbed plastic conduit, as close in diameter as possible to the exhaust pipe. Make up a roll of chicken wire or similar, thin enough to slide in the tube. Put it in (this is reinforcing for later) and have a can of expanding foam to hand.

Check the pipe does not obstruct the footpegs and the kickstart clears it. With it solidly locked in place, drill holes in the conduit the same diameter as the foam application tube. Having read the directions for the foam, fill the tube through the holes; do not go overboard, as the pressure from expanding foam is strong and could distort the conduit. Leave for a day, then remove carefully and clean off any overfill. You now have a 3D template to take to the tube benders.

Bits and Pieces

Making up the system will require access to a selection of ready-bent and straight tube pieces, which can be bought online. Alternatively, look for a decent local supplier, who may agree to refund you for any unused pieces. This will allow you to stock up with a good range to start with, rather than scrimping and possibly bodging.

Make sure that the bends are mandrel-bent, as this ensures the tube

reflect this. The usual practice is to have the header 'floating', with the silencer secured to the frame; anyone who has had headers on big singles and V-twins fracture would underline this strongly.

Making up a bespoke system is not too difficult, but it does need to be well planned and executed. First, identify the size of exhaust needed. Often, standard exhausts are smaller in bore than the custom version, and chunkier pipes always look good. If the size is

increased, then some jetting and tuning will be required.

One Piece

For a simple single-cylinder header, which needs to run down and along the frame below the engine, it is possible to make a mock-up and get it built at a specialist shop. This may sound expensive, but, as the shop will have all the equipment and skills to hand, there will keeps the same section and smooth lines. The wall thickness of the tube should be about 1.5mm and the outer diameters must match; sometimes they are labelled wrongly, so it is worth double-checking.

Start by putting the first piece into the exhaust port and wedging it solid. Fix the clamp in as well, then mount the silencer or tailpiece of the system in position; this gives a start and finish point.

Mock up the straight section(s) – it will help the lines of the bike if they run uphill to the tail, or at least horizontal. Exhausts that slope down look ungainly.

Now have a good look, take some measurements and lay out the system roughly on the floor to get an idea of where everything is going. The easiest way is to use a simple mix of bends that are connected on the straight runs. This means cuts will be more straightforward; cutting on a bend will result in an elliptical section that will need to be matched exactly on the next piece.

The first cut is the worst! Holding up the bend to the piece from the port,

For fancier systems, building the pipe up in situ is the way to go.

ABOVE: Bent tubes ready for cutting and joining.

RIGHT: The tube into the port is straight and can be cut after.

ABOVE: First sections tacked together for checking the positioning.
LEFT: Measuring the length to cut off and the sliding sleeve to distance.
BELOW: Mount in a vice and, with a fine cutting disc, using the sleeve end as a guide, calmly slice the pipe off. Deburr with a sanding disc on the outside and a round file or similar inside.

line up and mark the tube where it is to be cut. It may be necessary to cut both tubes to bring into place, so do this first.

Make a sleeve by cutting two lines along a short 75–125mm length of spare tube to knock out a 10mm strip and open it out so it is a tight slide fit on the pipe. If using larger-diameter tube, it needs to be squeezed down in the vice to do the same. Have some jubilee clips or exhaust clamps to tighten over this when it is in place on the pipe.

The short sleeve is also used to get a level cut, so it must be square at the end, which might take a bit of measuring and grinding to achieve. It is important to make sure you do this accurately. Take the piece to be cut and slide the sleeve on so that the true end lines up with the cut mark, and then tighten up the clamp.

Some builders will tack this together now, with the slot in the sleeve letting the welding rod get to the pipe. More cautious builders, such as myself, will have a number of sleeves, which allows the whole system to be built first, adjusted and then tacked. When it looks good and there is one tack on each section, loosen the sleeve and rotate it to put a tack at another point for strength. Carry on along until it is all done. The sleeves may need to be opened up to get them off, so do not become too attached to them.

Mounting Bolts

For single bolt mounts, get a large thick washer that fits over the head of a socket bolt of the right size. It may be necessary to grind or turn off some of the head for a good fit or to get the threaded part closer to the exhaust; leave a slight upstand on the head for the weld. Hammer the washer on a thick pipe or bar to give it a slight curve for sitting well on the pipe, and tack into place.

For two bolt mounts, which will give a steadier fix and repress vibration problems, do as above but use a section of tube wall, cut and shaped, with two holes in it. The reason for the washer flange is to spread out the stresses; if a nut is simply welded on, it can end up, through vibration, as a hole in the pipe.

Remount the piece and slide the sleeve to project halfway past the cut end and slide in the next (cut) piece to butt up.

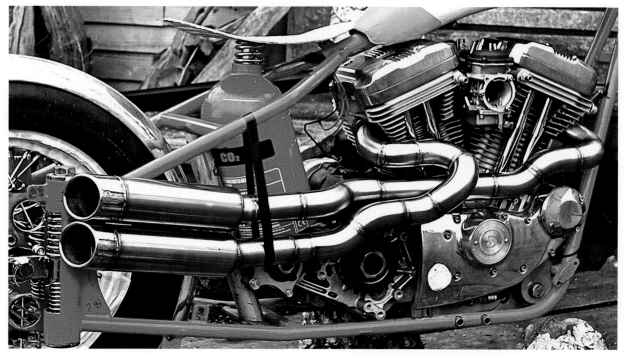

Get the pipe TIG-welded, telling the welder that it needs to penetrate completely to allow for cleaning off the visible welds. On some the weld is left to give character. This can be done with MIG or TIG.

ABOVE: Mounting bolt components.

RIGHT: A pair of classic Cherry Bomb silencers from production-car racing mated to pipes made with the plastic conduit method.

Screw-on clamps that compress the pipe into place, like these on an old Triumph, are prone to degradation. Use a thread file to spruce them up.

Clamps on exhausts often surrender through vibration and heat, so cannot be relied on in full; especially for competition machines or custom exhausts. Stainless-steel exhaust springs are used to hold the parts together, or the pipes into the head. These just need small tabs attached to both sides, further apart than the relaxed spring. When fitted, the spring absorbs vibration and the tension holds it all in place.

BAFFLED

An open-exhausted bike can sound glorious on full throttle, with the noise making it feel much faster to the rider. Unfortunately, not everyone will enjoy it as much as the custom biker and it may need to be quietened a bit to prevent a negative response. If a shop silencer is not your preference, there are alternatives: either build your own or insert baffles into the exhaust pipe. Baffles are metal tubes with holes and contours that slow down and reduce the noise of open pipes. They can be bought off the shelf and fixing is quite straightforward, by a bolt through the wall of the exhaust. Do not rely on a Nyloc nut to hold it for ever, as the heat will soften the plastic; use spring washers, stud locking and a second nut to lock it.

Other clamps have projecting studs to locate the clamp, fixed with a nut. As these are steel they always get a bit grotty, but can be neatened up by either replacing the stud with a stainless one, or removing and putting a stainless bolt through the clamp into the head. Check the threads on the stud, as they can sometimes differ at each end.

Use a new compressible exhaust washer, never an old one and pull the pipe into the port, but do not tighten up completely. Clamp the silencer in place and put a washer on to the mounting bolt, then fix through the mount with a washer and a spring washer before the nut. Get everything lying in a good position and then tighten up securely.

wiring and electrics

It is a serious reality check for any budding customizer, as their chosen bike is stripped of tank, seat and other outerwear, and the wiring loom is revealed: a thick black vine of crackling plastic running down the spine, sprouting multicoloured shoots to grubby little boxes and other components, wound around the frame, into the headlamp shell and out to the switches. Just removing this puzzling array without resorting to violence is a problem, while putting it back would seem to be an impossible task. Do not worry, however: it is feasible to dispense with this and simplify the electrics of a bike to a manageable level.

BASIC SYSTEM

Generic bike electrics are straightforward, with basically three parts to the system: charging, ignition and lighting/ancillaries.

Charging is from an alternator feeding AC current to a rectifier/regulator that feeds into the battery. On a simpler bike, the battery is sometimes dispensed with and all electric power comes direct from the alternator.

Ignition power comes from either the battery or the alternator and is fed to the coil, the points (or electronic system pack) break that circuit and the coil generates a high-voltage pulse through the spark plug.

Lights are powered from the alternator or battery by power coming in to the switches, which direct it to particular bulbs, travelling through (creating light) to reach ground (earth) and complete the circuit. When an electric starter is involved, this takes power from the battery to a solenoid (a heavy-duty switch) and when the starter is operated, this power is pushed into a rotating motor that turns the engine.

ABOVE RIGHT: Typical wiring condition of the 'well-maintained' classic buy.

RIGHT: The alternator: this version has an ignition pick-up that does not use points.

Into the mix are thrown a rectifier, to ensure the current to the battery is controlled, fuses to blow rather than components, and switches to connect or stop current flowing.

And that is it. Well, it is if your bike is from a time before the modern machines that have computerized control systems. Luckily, there are command packs that can be bought that will enable modern bikes to run on a simple system, but they can be pricey – sometimes as much as half the cost of the complete engine.

DESIGNING A SYSTEM

Designing a wiring system is basically the same for all bikes, but what will differ will be the location of components and their quality will vary.

First, purchase the components to be used, as these may be different from the original, and then figure out where to attach them on the bike. The battery is the main component – unless the build is going quite quickly, use an old one or a mock-up. Make its container and mount it prior to any painting or finishing, to allow all holes for wires or mounting components to be drilled.

The rectifier can be secured to the outside of the battery box, or in some other convenient place; if there are heat-sink or earthing requirements, ensure it is in contact with enough metal for this to be effective. As these are usually solid-state it is difficult to check on the operating condition, so if in doubt replace with a pattern part or one of the modern alternatives. It will also contain the regulator system; the rectifier changes the current from the alternator from alternating current (AC) to direct current (DC) and the regulator keeps the voltage correct for charging the battery.

Coils usually sit under the tank, so carry on with this if possible. Aftermarket coils may not fit the same brackets, so this will need to be sorted out at the frame mock-up stage, making sure that connections are accessible and not in contact with the frame and that HT leads have a clear run to the plugs.

Any other components, such as the ignition switch, engine-management systems, relays or ignition modules, need to be accounted for before the frame is finished. Construct the brackets and decide the cable routing at the mock-up stage as well.

Many a cool-looking bike has been built, looking clean and precise, only to have its lines ruined by a myriad of cables and wiring dangling all over the place. Obviously, the whole point of these is to join up parts of the bike or remotely control components, so they are needed, but they should be

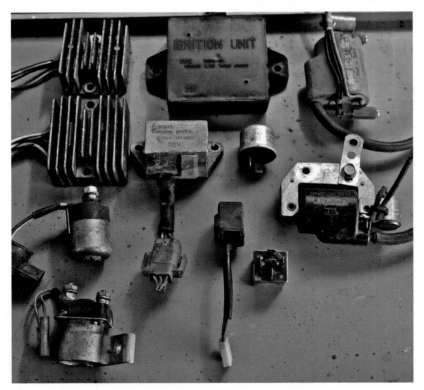

emergency light

If the bike is to be used at all times, there is a possibility that it could break down at night. To make this less of an ordeal, it is useful to have a light to see what needs to be fixed. Carry a head-mounted LED light, of the kind used by campers and fishermen, remembering to check battery levels regularly. One alternative is to have LEDs mounted at the brow of a helmet, with internal batteries.

TOP: If it cannot be hidden, make a feature of it. Battery and electric box made from the pump housing of a septic tank, in aluminium with some nice ribbing and details, switches inserted, sprayed black, and edges rubbed down. The rear light is made using the guts from an LED off-the-shelf piece inserted in an aluminium tube.

ABOVE: Typical electrical components of a bike: (top left) regulator/rectifiers; (bottom left) solenoids; (centre) relays and flasher; (right) coils; (top centre), ignition module.

condenser

The condenser will protect the points from too much pitting, but they can break down. At a pinch, any car or bike condenser should work.

Spark plugs with 'R' in the title have resistors and should not be used with plug caps that have resistors in.

When threading wires through handlebars or the frame, get a folded cable tie and push it into the exit hole so it expands to the inner walls. When the wire passes through, pull it out to snare the wire and bring it out.

kept tidy. Sit down and consider how this can be accomplished, remembering that complicated conduiting or concealment can spell trouble if anything goes wrong and access is needed. The competent builder will bring all these details together in a unified form, rather than slapping it on as an afterthought.

Once the components are all in place, it is possible to start running the wiring to them and minimizing their presence. Conversely, if you cannot hide it, make the routing sharp and organized, and apply as much thought to its presence as to anything else on the bike.

SKETCHING A LAYOUT

Once you have established exactly which components are needed to make the bike road legal, it is the time to draw a diagram. Roughly sketch a schematic layout of the bike, showing where each component goes. Next, from the battery work outwards until everything is connected up with a wire that brings power to it, and, if needed, an earth out. Insert all the fuses needed and any relays, trying to keep them in a place that is logical in terms of access and preferably not too far away from the power source. There are many basic diagrams for custom wiring available on the internet; do a search and find one that is close to your needs, adding or deleting components as required.

Use a colour code in the wiring system that makes sense, especially if the bike is to be sold later, or if it needs work when the diagram is not to hand. Be aware that the wires that come attached to components may not be regularized so you may need to test the circuit to find out which is power, and so on.

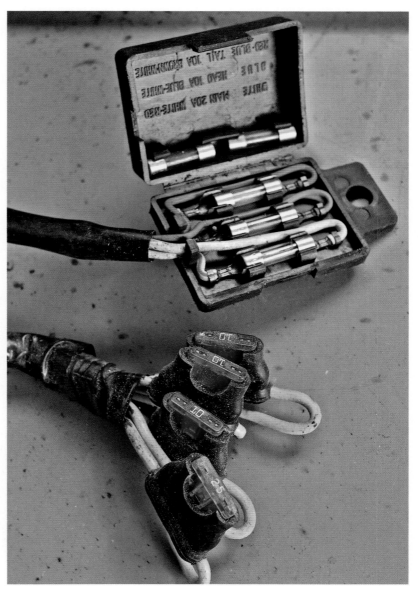

Glass tube fuses and blade fuses.

Types of Fuse

There are two types of fuse. The old-school version is a glass tube with a wire running through it. The advantages are that the holders are thin and often weatherproof, and can be spliced in anywhere and easily tucked out of site. On the downside, they are a bit fragile to rattle around in the spares tin. Nowadays, blade fuses are the sensible choice. They need a dedicated housing box, which is a bit lumpy, but they are practical for controlling the layout. They are also easier to find in general motoring shops, and cheap and robust when carried as spares.

A minimum of four fuses will be needed on a simple 12V bike. Roughly, these work out as: main from battery 25/30 amp, ignition about 5 amp, auxiliaries about 10 amps and lights about 15 amps.

If there are other items and you need to put more power through, then it is fairly simple to work out the size of fuse needed, knowing that amps = watts/volts.

So add up the wattage of the items to be installed – for example, 20-watt horn plus 20-watt brake light plus indicators (two bulbs and relay, total 50 watts) – and divide by 12(V).

Take the total wattage of 90 divided by 12 (7.5), add about 10 per cent over, and round up to a 10-amp fuse. Do not go too high with the rating, though – if the fuse is not the weakest link, wires can melt and bulbs can blow.

Connections and Connectors

It is tempting to use long uninterrupted wires from one end of the bike to the other. As most wiring is put in last thing on custom bikes, it would be simple to do and in reality make for a stronger system. However, the downside comes when work is to be done and parts have to be removed. In this case, it is best to have connections that allow the bike to be dismantled easily, with each part's wiring connected at a suitable point.

The quality of the connectors is paramount in ensuring good current flow and longevity; once the system has been designed and work has begun,

use the best type of connector available. At the low end of the market, you will find a press-on type that cuts through the wire and holds it in place with the other wire. It is a little blue box with a clip-down securing mechanism and, apart from an emergency repair on the go, it should never be used.

At the next level up, there are ready-insulated connecters, on which the stripped end of the wire is fed into an alloy tube surrounded by plastic or silicon insulation, then crimped up. They are usually sold in DIY shops and retail motor factors. They usually fail to hold properly and will let you down, so, again, they should not be used except as a get-you-home solution.

The best option for single-wire connections are plain metal connectors of the same size and design as used by the bike manufacturers, where the stripped wire is crimped and held both on the bare wire and its plastic outer. These are then covered and insulated by sliding a silicon sheath over or by using heat-shrink tube.

For joining one group of wires to another group, a block connecter is the

Crimped connectors over soldered wire. When joining a bundle of wires, stagger the connections so that they lie flat; it also helps to prevent bunching up when threading through bars.

ABOVE: *Get these types of crimp connector, in spade, bullet and eye options; use with correct crimping pliers and build up a stock by buying in batches of fifty.*

RIGHT: *The good and bad: Deutsch connector and emergency connection boxes.*

earthing out

Any wire with power running through is live and will short if it touches a metal part of the bike. When putting on connectors, always use the female for power out (live) lines, with the insulated sheaths preventing contact with metal when working on the system.

The earth for the headlight components should be carried back to the frame, not to the headlamp shell. The battery earth should be attached to the frame and, if necessary, put an earth from the frame to the engine.

splicing wires

LEFT: *Splicing wires: cut and expose the inner.*

BELOW LEFT: *Slide together so the wires interlace, then twist together.*

BELOW RIGHT: *Heat with soldering iron and feed in solder until the wire is coated. If using flux, apply beforehand.*

BOTTOM: *Let it cool, and slide heat-shrink over and seal.*

The tidy wiring layout under the seat of Jen's SR500, using cable ties and ribbed sheath, with the components secured so they can be accessed easily. A layout like this makes life simple when trying to trace faults.

best option. These range from simple plastic boxes (Molex type), which are acceptable in protected areas, to Weatherpack or Deutsch connectors, which are what sensible people use. These are weatherproof, can be reused and will make the set-up look very professional. Original connectors off the old wiring harness can be used – they will lock on to the standard components properly – but this may involve lots of splicing or more connections.

Wire

Vehicle wire is composed of strands of copper wound together. The thicker the wire, the more amps can go through it. Never use house-style single-core wire on a bike, as it will eventually vibrate and shear off, usually somewhere cold, dark and wet.

The right wire has a plastic covering to prevent contact and this should not have any breaks or nicks in it. Thicker wires, for starter motors and earth, are called cables.

For most applications, 8-amp maximum rated wire is good enough, while battery cables need to be rated higher, at 20/30 amps.

MAKING UP THE SYSTEM

First, all the electric components need to be secured to their position on the bike; make sure that connectors are not

curly cable

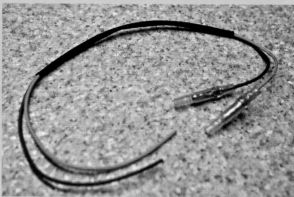

TOP LEFT: *Rather than have listless wires draped to components, sharpen it up with neat coils.*

TOP RIGHT: *Slide heat-shrink over wires that are going to be exposed and need to flex, such as those at the headstock.*

ABOVE RIGHT: *Wrap tightly coiled around a bolt and heat up the heat-shrink, then hold in place until cool.*

RIGHT: *The neat result stops sagging wire.*

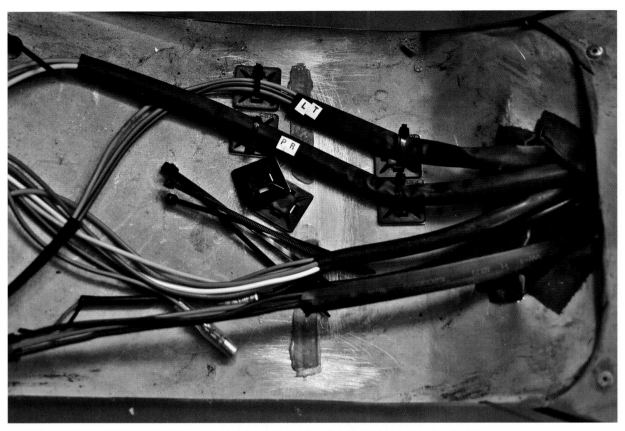

Stick-on cable tie bases are handy for locating and holding down wires. Marking the wires makes it easier when checking.

going to short on metal or be pinched by covers. For areas at risk of crushing or chafing, buy some adhesive-backed foam to pad and protect the vulnerable bit.

Using masking tape, start attaching wires to the bike frame roughly as per your wiring diagram; make sure the colours of the wires are noted on the diagram. Allow extra length past components, especially at the headlight to frame area; this needs to let the front end turn completely, so give it room. Put on heat-shrink or cable wraps as required, but leave loose until all is finished, as changes may occur. Fix connectors on to the wires and attach to the components in one area, then clip the bundle to its final position nearest to this area. Now the loom can be pulled into position as you work towards other parts of the bike and secured with cable ties if you are sure that it is right, or taped to allow for adjustment. If in doubt, always settle for a bit of slack rather than pulled tight in the runs.

TESTING

Once everything is joined up, it is time to test the circuits. Rather than turning the bike on and finding out that there are faults as a result of nothing happening, or fuses blowing, you can check beforehand that there is continuity within the loom. Is the power getting from start (battery/alternator) to finish (lights, horn, and so on)? Use a multimeter or circuit tester to find out. Start at the power connector on the loom and check to see if there is a circuit to the component. If there is not (and you have turned the switch to 'on'), work outwards from the source through the joins and components until the circuit is made. Fix the issue and try again.

On painted handlebars make sure, if using a button kill switch, that there is bare metal for it to ground on; if necessary, clean off using a wire brush in a drill.

Once all seems to be good, attach the battery and try out everything, one at a time first, then all together or in combinations to check that one does not cut out another. If possible, start the bike and make sure the system is not affected by vibration or power surges.

Possibly the most common fault with shed-built electrics is grounding (earthing), usually because there is not a good earth for the components. Battery terminals have a habit of coming loose, so always check this first. The second likely problem is unintentional earthing, which means a short in the system from frayed or interconnecting wires. Never put wiring through a hole or between two moving parts without extra layer(s) of protection.

LIGHTS, INSTRUMENTS AND HORNS

Bulbs

The first criteria for a bike headlight is bulb wattage – if it is too low, there will not be enough illumination; if it is too high, it may draw too much power or there will not be enough to get the best result. Check the manual to see which bulbs are recommended.

Luckily, most fittings are universal, allowing variations to be used.

Developments in bulbs, LED and optics have led to some good alternatives to the standard, although other items such as relays may need to be fitted. As each bike has specific needs, the advice here is to do some research, checking forums and consulting with responsible dealers. It is important to get the best. Cheap light sources are likely to let you down and, when you are riding a bike at night, you do not want this to happen. A cool-looking light that costs peanuts could prove to be a mistake, so do not be tempted.

Two recycled lights: (left) one from an old army vehicle, with the clips as part of the design; a new rim was turned from aluminium and a sealed-beam light unit was used; and (right) a 1930s car headlight shell, which has a powerful car set-up fixed inside and a classic bike lens to cover; the finish is the original nickel-plating, lightly rubbed with wire wool, then clear-lacquered.

The future of biking? An electric-powered bike with a ring of LEDs for daylight riding.

Housing

It is possible to use unusual head-lamp shells found in some old scrap-yard or similar, but modern units may be incompatible with them. There is a huge range of new, replacement and custom units available, so the decision is yours. If you decide to go for new, choose a reputable manufacturer, as knock-offs may be from countries that do not need to adhere to your country's regulations, or do not care.

Mounting will be by brackets attached to the fork legs or by bolt-ing on to the yokes. For ease, the stan-chion brackets will be best, so a shell with two side fixings will be required. Mounting off the yokes can require the drilling and tapping of bolt holes, or the permanent attachment of tabs, and these are operations that may need to be carried out at the design stage. It may be too difficult to incor-porate them into the existing set-up. Once again, planning out before con-struction is the best option.

There should be enough room in the shell to accommodate the wires and possibly relays. Wires need to be long enough, allowing the lens or bulb to be dismounted and checked while still connected. Try to label the wires for checking systems. Ensure they have good insulation and that any holes through metal have grommets or simi-lar to prevent chafing. Remember to run an earth from the shell or electri-cal components to the frame; do not rely on current getting through on its own. When putting everything togeth-er, make sure the wires do not get trapped and take care not to pull off the connections.

TOP LEFT: *Typical headlight interior. Make sure the connections for the bars and the main bike are all contained within the shell.*
LEFT: *Headlight mounts should be secure, as vibration can loosen them and cause problems; use rubber sleeves and compressible washers. This generic pair bought online had the paint polished off and my usual treatment of randomly drilled holes, harking back to the style of old café racers. It is cheap and easy to do, and gives a good result.*

Beam Alignment

When everything has been mounted, you need to check that the headlight beam is at the correct height and alignment. To do this, find a blank wall with plenty of room in front of it, then get a friend to sit on the bike and measure the height of the bulb from the floor. Mark this as a line on the wall – this is the Horizontal Zero Line – then draw a vertical line through this, projecting above about 400mm, as the Vertical Zero Line. Touch the VZL with the front wheel and wheel back to 3.8 metres.

If the HZL is less than 850mm, the top cut-off of the dip beam should be about 50mm below the HZL. If it is taller than 850mm, it should be about 75mm below.

Full beam should kick up about 100mm from the VZL to prevent dazzle.

Running

Start the engine and turn on the lights, rev a bit and see if the light flickers (allowing for vibration of the bike). If it does, check the connections throughout first, then the switch contact points. If it increases with revs, there could be a battery charge issue. For bikes without batteries there will be some fluctuation with the revs; just make sure there is a constant enough base for illumination. It may be necessary to check the alternator, and you might want to consider one of the charging upgrades that are available for some bikes.

It is possible to run lights direct from the alternator, but this power can fluctuate and blow bulbs; if this happens, use a higher-wattage bulb, not a stronger fuse!

Rear Lights

LEDs are preferable for rear lights, as they do not drain power, can be smaller and, if done properly, will outlast bulbs. One issue is that, as the light emitted does not expand like a bulb and can therefore be harder to see, you will need to use as many as you can stuffed into the light housing. Once again, buy the best quality you can – manufacturers of LEDs tend to flog off the lower quality cheaply and these can end up in bargain bins.

Brake Lights

Being seen is important to bikers, and not just because they like showing off – it could save a life. Visible brake lights are not just a legal obligation, they are necessary to prevent rear-end shunts, so make sure that they work. A switch will be needed for this. Old school used to be a small item operated by the action of the rear brake lever pulling a spring, or with a hydraulic switch in the brake line. These are fiddly to mount and maintain, usually put in at the very end of construction, almost as an

afterthought. It is preferable to use the front brake to activate it, which is easily done, as most hydraulic levers have a tiny switch incorporated into the component. This set-up is much more useful, as it is the front brake that is used most often.

When wiring the bulb up alongside the rear light, make the brake light the brighter of the two elements, as it must outshine the rear and be visible in daylight. Adhesive LED strips can be wired in as brake lights, mounted along rear loops, surrounding number plates or on mudguards. Make the connections

LEFT: *Crusty old light recycled on the back of a well-worn chop; a new light would have looked ridiculous.*

BELOW: *Universal aftermarket taillight; simple and easy to get hold off, it works well with a wide range of styles.*

Old lights from scrapyards and farmyards all have the potential to be recycled as interesting features.

Old clocks and (centre bottom) the modern alternative, a motorcycle computer that shows speed in km/h or mph, distance and time travelled, and a rev counter.

waterproof and secure the wires, and you should end up with a neat solution.

Indicators

Turn signals represent another layer of complication, so they are not always incorporated. If they are required, however, there are many styles and sizes available. Once again, LED is now the obvious choice, although they do need to have a power regulator in place, as the flasher relay relies on a certain power take-off to work correctly – this is why indicators will flash rapidly when a bulb in the system is burnt out.

Horn

The horn is another legal requirement, and often as not a late addition to the build. It will require a secure mounting and wire out. Using recycled switches can result in there being no button – if a starter or kill button is not being used, try converting it to operate the horn, as the wiring is similar. A good spot is underneath the yokes or just below the front of the tank. The connections are prone to corrosion and need to be weatherproofed and well contacted.

The fiddly nature of spade connections makes it handy to have good access, as they can come adrift easily. The light finish on cheap ones leads to rapid grubbiness. Retro covers can be sourced online or in scrapyards; if they are still in good condition, that indicates good-quality materials.

Clocks

Speedo and rev counters can now be bought as an integrated unit. The wiring and set-up instructions are easy enough to follow, although the mounting of magnetic pick-ups and associated wiring can be awkward on a finished build. Classic bikes have a mechanical activation that is driven off the wheel hub; these can be quite neglected and will need refurbishing. Issues are different-diameter wheels, which alter the calibration, and the need for a compatible speedo that might not be suited to the style. Do some homework to reduce any potential problems.

Cheap units can be mounted in neater bodies. The simplest way is to turn up one from aluminium tube.

Riding bikes is great fun, and building your own ride is a satisfying accomplishment that can be the start of a lifelong passion. Just make sure that it is a long life. This means not doing anything dangerous or radically over the top to a machine that could be a death trap if it is not constructed correctly. Make sure it is maintained well and always capable of coping with the rigours of life in the fast lane. Talk to other riders and builders, listen to advice and do not be afraid to ask questions. Being a shed builder is a continuous learning process.

This book is a guide to turning an average bike into something special, show bikes are a different matter entirely. The wild creations seen at meets and online can often be unridable day to day. Expensively painted, uncomfortable and idiosyncratic, they will not offer their owner half as much fun as hammering around on a well-prepared bike used as the basis for creative modifications.

The point of this book: getting it built and getting out there…

glossary

Aftermarket Part made for bike but not OEM

Air-cooled Using fins to radiate heat off the engine rather than liquid in a radiator

Airbox Container holding the air filter, usually mounted under the seat

Airhead (Boxer) Older air-cooled BMW twin

Allen key Tool for socket-head bolts

Alloy A mixture of two or more metals

Aluminium (aluminum) Alloy metal offering ease of working, lightness and anti-corrosion properties

Anodizing Coating metal (aluminium) with a coloured oxide to look good and reduce corrosion

Ape-hangers Very high handlebars

Axle (spindle) Shaft for wheel to rotate around

Ayjay AJS bike

Baffle(r) Plate to slow down gas in an exhaust system

Banjo fitting Metal component attached to tube for oil or hydraulic fluid that has a bolt placed through it

Barrels (jugs, pots) Cylinders of engine

Bars Handlebars

Basket case Bike in bits ready to start work on

Beemer BMW bike

Beezer BSA bike

Belt drive (rubber band) Alternative to chain, using a toothed belt to transmit power

Big twin Large-capacity V-twin bike

Blinkers (indicators, flashers) Flashing lights to show which way you are turning

Blower (supercharger) Mechanical means of forcing fuel/air into engine

Boots (rubber, knobblies, slicks) Tyres

Bowden cable Control cable for brakes etc

Brake bleeding Ridding the hydraulic system of air to make brakes work efficiently

Brake pad Set inside caliper for disc brakes

Brake shoe Curved plate with brake material on for use with a drum brake

Bump start Push start

Burr Rough edge on metal after cutting or wear

Bush Liner for a bearing or a pivot

Cable ties Plastic or metal strips used to tie around and hold in place

Caliper Brake component that sits astride a disc

Carb Carburettor

Carbon fibre (carbon) Plastic that is light, strong and expensive, used for bodywork and some components

Carburettor (carb) Component that controls air and fuel for engine

Cast wheel Alloy wheel

Chain pitch Size of chain

Chair Sidecar

Chassis Frame and suspension of a bike

Chrome Shiny metallic coating by electrolysis

Circlip Metal clip that sits in a groove and holds pieces on or in a shaft

Clip-ons Handlebars for café racers that are attached to the stanchions

Clocks Speedometer & rev counter

Clubman bars Handlebars that angle down for café racers

Coil Component for creating a high-voltage surge to the spark plug

Contact patch (footprint) The part of a tyre that touches the road

Counterbore Recess to allow head of bolt to sit in

Cowhorns Wide, raised and swept-back handlebars

Crash bars Tube frames used to protect engine

Damper Component to reduce vibration, fitted in end of bars

Disc brake Brake where the action is used to grip a disc

Displacement The size of an engine in cubic centimetres (cc) or cubic inches (in)

Down tubes Frame tubes running in front of engine from headstock

Drag bars Straight handlebars

Drum brake Brake where the shoes work inside the hub

Dual sport Cross-country race/bike for on- and off-road riding

Electronic ignition Electronic control for spark-plug firing

Enduro (dirt bike) Trail bike

Engine (lump) Motor

Ergonomics A way of building things that suit the way a human body works

Expansion chamber Part of two-stroke exhaust to increase power

Fasteners Nuts and bolts

Filter Mesh or paper that prevents dirt and grit travelling to vulnerable areas in oil or fuel

Final drive Power delivery to the back wheel, via chain, belt or shaft

Flashers (blinkers, indicators) Flashing lights to show which way you are turning

Fork brace Fitted across forks to reduce flexing

Fork clamps Yokes

Fork legs Front fork legs

Fork sliders Tube into which stanchions fit

Forks Front suspension

Four-stroke Engine with mechanical valves with four actions: induction; compression; combustion; exhaust

Front end Forks and front wheel

Fuel injection Instead of carbs, method by which fuel is injected direct to the engine

Fuse Electrical component that melts if overloaded, preventing damage to components

Galling When stainless-steel fasteners seize up during installation

Gasket Paper or copper shape compressed between components to create a seal

Gearhead Keen vehicle lover

Girder Front suspension

Grips (handlebar grips) Rubber or leather tubes over ends of handlebars for holding on to and operating throttle

Grub screw (set screw) Bolt threaded all the way along with a recessed socket or slot

Hardtail (rigid back end) Frame type with no rear suspension

Headers Downpipes

Highway pegs Footpegs mounted to allow feet to rest on when cruising

Hub Centre of a wheel

Hugger Close-fitting mudguard

Indicators (blinkers, flashers) Flashing lights to show which way you are turning

Inline four Engine that has four cylinders in a row

Ironhead Type of Harley Sportster

Jet Brass carb fitting that delivers precise volumes of fuel

Jubilee clip (hose clip) Metal ring that is tightened around a rubber tube to hold it in place

K&N Air filter manufacturer, now a generic name for this style of filter, with pleated surface that sits directly on carb

Kick stand Side stand

Knobblies Tyres used on dirt bikes

Kwacker Kawasaki bike

LED Light-emitting diode, used as an alternative to glass bulbs

Lid Crash helmet

Lock nut (jam nut) Thin nut used to tighten against another to prevent loosening

Loctite Liquid applied to thread to prevent loosening

Mag Alloy wheel made in one piece

Mike Micrometer

Mill Unit used to power bike

Mock-up Set-up prior to construction, to see how components will fit or look

Monocoque Sheet-metal all-in-one construction (often frame)

Monoshock Rear suspension that uses one shock absorber

Mudguard (fender) Curved cowl over tyres to prevent spray and dirt hitting rider or bike

Neck Location of steering head

Nyloc nut Nut with nylon insert to grip on bolt and prevent loosening

O-ring Rubber ring used for sealing around bolt or shaft or two mating surfaces

OEM (Original Equipment Manufacturer) Term used to designate components that come as standard on or for a particular bike

OHC Overhead-cam engine

Oil cooler Radiator through which engine oil flows to help cooling

Oilhead Late-model BMW using oil to cool engine

Outfit (combo, chair) Motorbike and sidecar

Pattern parts Copies of OEM parts

Pegs Footpegs

Perch The mount on a handlebar where a control lever is fixed

Petcock (Petrol/gas tap) Valve to control fuel flow

Phosphor bronze A hard-wearing alloy used for bearing surfaces

Pipes Exhaust pipe from the cylinder to the silencer

Pitch Distance between tops of thread on bolt, measured in imperial by teeth per inch (TPI). Can be fine or coarse depending on application

Plug gap Distance between electrodes of a spark plug

Points Contacts that open on a cam, breaking the current to a coil, thus activating it

Polarity Which terminal of battery is earthed and which power

Primary drive Power delivery from engine to gearbox, via the clutch

Rake Angle of forks to vertical

Rat bike Unwashed, uncared for and often surprisingly reliable bike

Rattle can Paint supplied in a pressurized spray can

Rear loop Subframe that supports seat and mudguard

Rearsets Footpegs and controls set further back than standard

Rectifier Component that changes AC from alternator to DC for use in lights, ignition, and so on

Relay box A switch that reduces power surges for components

Rigid frame Frame with no rear suspension

Rim Outer part of a wheel in which the tyre sits

Risers Mounts of various design and height/pullback for attaching handlebars

Rolling chassis Motorbike minus the engine

Rolling gear Wheels

Rolling start Pushing a bike in gear to start it

Scraping (banking, leaning, carving) Leaning hard into a corner

Seal Rings, usually of rubber and sometimes with wire inserts, to prevent ingress of dirt on shafts and stanchions

Seat base Underside of seat

Seat hump Bodywork behind seat

Shim Metal plate or washer of exact size for spacing

Shock absorbers (shocks, shox) Rear suspension units

Shotgun pipes Exhausts that terminate together, straight cut and in line

Silencers Items attached to exhaust headers to provide back pressure and reduce noise

Skid lid Helmet, open or full-face

Slop Construction that is not a rigid as it should be

Socket head (Allen bolt) Bolt with a hexagonal recess

Solvol Polishing paste for aluminium and chrome

Spoked wheel Wheel that has a hub and rim joined by tightened metal rods (spokes)

Springer Front suspension

Stainless steel Steel alloy resistant to corrosion

Stanchions Fork tubes

Steering damper Piston and tube component attached to forks and frame to hold front end steady when riding

Steering lock The amount the front end can be turned

Stroker Two-stroke bike

Subframe Frame area that does not hold engine

Swarfega Hand-cleaning gel

Swing arm Arm or fork that holds the rear wheel and can move up and down

Tank slapper When handlebars start oscillating at speed, due to wheel issues or frame set-up

Tap/Tapping Threaded cutter/cutting a thread on the inside of a hole or nut

Terminal Point at which wire connects to electrical component or battery

Throttle (twist grip) Control to let more air into a carburettor

Thumper Big single four-stroke

Tread Pattern cut into a tyre

Tribsa Triumph in BSA frame

Triton Triumph in Norton frame

Trummy/Trumpet Triumph bike

Tunnel Underside of petrol tank that sits over frame

Twin leading shoe Drum brake where the shoes are pushed out at both ends

Twinshock Rear suspension using a pair of shock absorbers

Two into one Exhaust pipe where the two pipes join together into one

Two-stroke Engine where intake and exhaust are combined, so combustion happens every other stroke

UJM Universal Japanese machine; description of similar-styled bikes of the 1970s and 1980s

Unsprung weight Anything that is attached to the moving end of suspension

USD forks (inverted forks) Forks that have stanchions at the wheel end

VIN (frame number, engine number) Vehicle identification number, used for paperwork and protection

Vintage bike Classic bike that is more than twenty years old

WD40 Spray for dispersing moisture and penetrating corroded parts

Wheelbase Distance between centre of front and rear wheels

Wiring loom/harness The rope of wires that carry power to and from electrical components along the bike

Wrench (grease monkey) Mechanic

Yam (Jamjar) Yamaha bike

Yokes Triple tree

Zorst Sporty exhaust

index

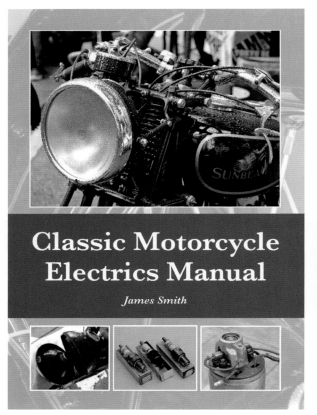
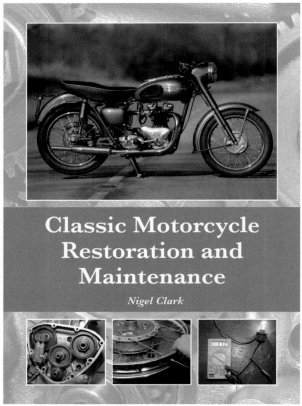